Crossroads Café
PARTNER GUIDE

Elizabeth Minicz

HEINLE & HEINLE PUBLISHERS

An International Thomson Publishing Company

Boston, Massachusetts 02116 U.S.A.

New York • London • Bonn • Boston • Detroit • Madrid • Melbourne • Mexico City • Paris •
Singapore • Tokyo • Toronto • Washington • Albany, NY • Belmont, CA • Cincinnati, OH

The publication of *Crossroads Café* was directed by the members of the Heinle & Heinle Secondary and Adult ESL Publishing Team.

Senior Editorial Director: Roseanne Mendoza
Senior Production Services Coordinator: Lisa McLaughlin
Market Development Director: Jonathon Boggs

Also participating in the publication of the program were:

Vice President and Publisher, ESL: Stanley Galek
Developmental Editor: Sally Conover
Production Editor: Maryellen Killeen
Manufacturing Coordinator: Mary Beth Hennebury
Full Service Design and Production: PC&F, Inc.

Manufactured in the United States of America.

ISBN: 0-8384-66141

Heinle & Heinle is a division of International Thomson Publishing, Inc.

WHAT'S IN THIS PARTNER GUIDE?

The questions and answers that follow will help you use the *Partner Guide*. The *Partner Guide* offers you ideas for helping learners speak English! Pages 2–10 will give you ideas for using the *Photo Stories* and the *Worktexts*. Pages 11–44 offer specific ideas for using the *Worktexts*.

WHO IS A PARTNER?

A *partner*

◆ is someone a learner can talk to in English.
◆ helps a learner study regularly.
◆ helps a learner have fun while learning English.

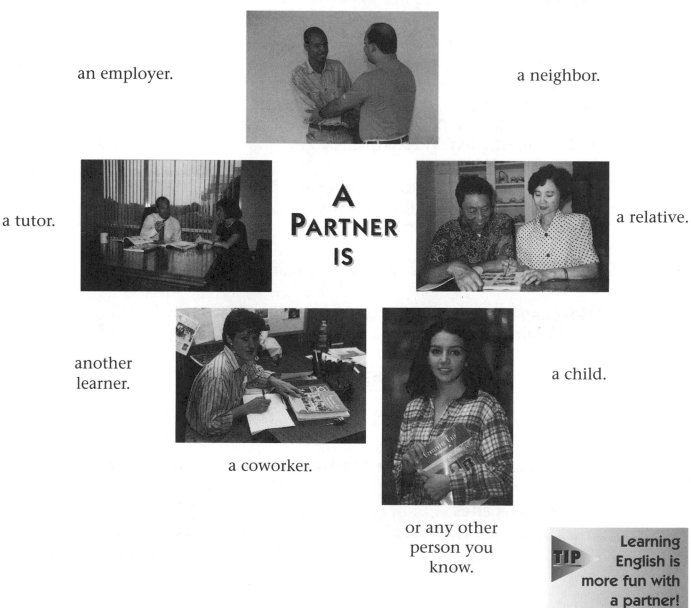

a friend.

an employer.

a neighbor.

a tutor.

A PARTNER IS

a relative.

another learner.

a child.

a coworker.

or any other person you know.

TIP Learning English is more fun with a partner!

WHAT DO I NEED TO BE A PARTNER?

◆ enthusiasm
◆ interest
◆ a desire to help
◆ patience
◆ time
◆ instructional materials
◆ a place to meet

WHAT CAN A PARTNER DO?

help the
learner speak
English.

check
learner
progress.

A PARTNER CAN

meet
regularly
with the
learner.

use ideas from
this book.

TIP Speak English as much as possible. But don't be afraid to translate, if you can, when you need to.

WHAT'S THE DIFFERENCE BETWEEN A TUTOR AND A PARTNER?

Tutors are partners, too, but with a difference. Tutors are often volunteers. They are usually trained by literacy programs, community organizations, or schools to work with learners. Some tutors work one-on-one with learners. Some tutors work with small groups of learners. Some tutors work in classrooms with teachers. And some tutors work in libraries, learning centers, or even learners' homes. This *Partner Guide* is useful for all kinds of tutors!

Here are some activities tutors may want to do.

◆ Watch the *Crossroads Café* videos with learners if they can.
◆ Review *Worktext* lessons.
◆ Help learners converse.
◆ Help learners understand new vocabulary.
◆ Help learners with pronunciation.
◆ Use the Blackline Masters that are purchased separately.
◆ Help learners read and write.

TIP ▶ Ask learners what they want to do!

WHERE DOES A LEARNER WATCH THE *CROSSROADS CAFÉ* VIDEOS?

at home.

in a classroom.

A LEARNER CAN WATCH THE VIDEOS

at a community center.

at a library.

HOW CAN A PARTNER HELP A LEARNER WATCH THE VIDEOS?

Before a learner watches the videos,

◆ encourage her* to watch the videos as many times as possible.

◆ explain to the learner that she doesn't have to understand every word. She will understand a lot by watching the characters' actions and paying attention to their facial expressions, gestures, and body language.

While the learner watches the video, she should think about the **Focus for Watching** questions in the *Worktext*.

◆ What is the story about?

◆ What are the characters' names?

After the learner watches the videos, ask questions like the following or make up your own before you go over the **After You Watch** pages in the *Worktext*.

◆ Tell me what happened?

◆ Who are the characters?

◆ Has anything like this happened to you?

◆ Which character in the story do you like the most? the least? Why?

> **TIP** Encourage the learner to watch the videos as many times as possible.

HOW CAN A PARTNER HELP A LEARNER USE THE *PHOTO STORIES?*

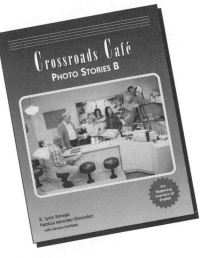

1. Discuss the unit opener page and ask questions such as:

◆ Who do you see?

◆ What are they doing?

◆ What are they saying?

◆ What does the title mean?

* **Note:** Both singular and plural pronouns are used to refer to learners in the *Partner Guide. She* is used to refer to a single learner because it is too awkward to say *he* or *she*.

2. Talk about the photos in the *Photo Stories* and ask questions such as:

   ◆ Is Mr. Brashov a cook?
   ◆ Is Mr. Brashov angry or sad?
   ◆ What is Mr. Brashov doing?
   ◆ What is Mr. Brashov saying? thinking?

3. Ask the learner to ask you questions about the *Photo Stories* such as:

   Learner: What is Jamal doing?
   Partner: He's walking on the sidewalk.

4. Review new vocabulary. Point to various words. Ask the learner to say each word, define it, spell it, and use it in a sentence.

5. Help the learner write language experience stories about the episode. See page 8 for more information about language experience stories.

TIP Before you turn each page in the *Photo Stories*, ask the learner what she thinks will happen next.

HOW CAN A PARTNER USE THE VIDEO SUMMARIES?

The video summaries tell the stories shown in the video episodes. The summaries start on page 45 of this guide.

Step #1   Have the learner read the whole summary silently as quickly as possible.

Step #2   Ask the learner questions about the summary. Here are some examples.

◆ Is Rosa a chef? (yes/no question)
◆ Is Rosa a chef or a waitress? (either/or question)
◆ What is Rosa's job? (questions using what, where, when, why, how, how long)

Step #3   Have the learner read the summary silently while you read it aloud.

Step #4   Have the learner read the summary aloud. Reading aloud helps learners with pronunciation.

Optional Activities Using the Summaries:

Write 7–10 sentences from the summary on small paper strips. Mix up the strips. Have the learner read the strips to you, then put them in order.

Write 3–5 true sentences and 3–5 false sentences about the summary on small strips of paper. Scramble the strips. Ask the learner to read each sentence then decide if it is true or false. Have the learner find the true sentences in the summary and correct the false ones.

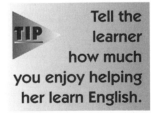

TIP Read the summary if you don't have time to watch the video before you meet with the learner.

HOW CAN A PARTNER HELP A LEARNER STAY MOTIVATED TO LEARN ENGLISH?

◆ Talk about when and where the learner is studying.
◆ Encourage the learner to continue studying.
◆ Review previous lessons.
◆ Ask the learner to retell the stories.
◆ Discuss each of the characters.
◆ Ask the learner to tell you what she has learned.
◆ Ask the learner if she wants to do anything different when you meet.
◆ Review the **Ways to Learn** and **Record Your Progress** charts in the *Worktexts* with the learner.

TIP Tell the learner how much you enjoy helping her learn English.

WHAT ELSE CAN A PARTNER DO?

Encourage the learner to practice speaking, reading, and writing English as much as possible. Here are some ideas to use when you meet with the learner.

Write in a Journal

Step #1	Ask the learner to buy a spiral notebook for journal writing.
Step #2	Tell the learner to write about anything she is interested in related to the Crossroads Café stories.
Step #3	Read the learner's journal frequently and write several sentences or questions about the entries.
Step #4	Don't make corrections unless the learner asks you to do so.
Step #5	Discuss journal entries with the learner.

Dictate Sentences to the Learner

Dictation is a good way to practice several English skills simultaneously—the learner listens, writes, and reads sentences in English. Try to do a dictation exercise every time you meet. Here are some suggestions.

Step #1	Choose 3–5 short, simple sentences from the *Worktexts* or *Photo Stories*.
Step #2	Tell the learner to listen to the first sentence, but not write it.
Step #3	Repeat the sentence. Tell the learner how many words are in the sentence.
Step #4	Give the learner time to write the sentence.
Step #5	Repeat the sentence if needed.
Step #6	Show the learner where to find the sentences in the *Worktext* or *Photo Story*.
Step #7	Have the learner correct the dictation.

> **TIP** Encourage learners to correct their own errors.

Write Language Experience Stories

Step #1	Ask the learner to look at a photo from the learning materials or think about a part or whole story.
Step #2	Have the learner talk about the photo or story.
Step #3	Write what the learner says.
Step #4	Read the learner's words to her.
Step #5	Ask the learner if she wants to make any changes or corrections.
Step #6	Read the story aloud while the learner follows along.
Step #7	Point to words and sentences and have the learner read them to you.
Step #8	Have the learner practice reading the story as many times as she is interested.

Discuss Current Events or Community Activities Related to the Topics in the Videos

Step #1   Listen to the radio or television for stories about topics in the videos.

Step #2   Ask the learner if she heard or saw the story.

Step #3   Talk about the story and relate it to Crossroads Café.

Read and Discuss Magazine and Newspaper Stories Related to the Topics in the Videos

Step #1   Ask the learner to look in newspapers or magazines for stories related to the videos, or bring newspapers and magazines to your meetings and look through them together for stories related to the videos.

Step #2   Use the techniques on page 7 for reading together.

TIP Relate the video stories to the learner's life whenever possible.

GUIDE FOR USING THE UNIT NOTES

To the Partner: Read the next two pages **before** you use the **Unit Notes.** These pages will show you how to use the **Unit Notes** to help learners who are using the *Worktexts* to practice speaking English. Use the sample questions and conversation ideas in these notes with the photos and activities in every unit of the *Worktexts*.

Unit Opener

1. Talk about the photo on the first page of the unit in the *Worktext*. Point to the picture and ask the learner:

   ◆ Who are these people?
   ◆ Where are they?
   ◆ What are they doing?

2. Ask the learner to complete the **Ways to Learn** section below the opening photo. Talk about the learner's responses.

Before You Watch

Note: In each unit, the underlined words will change.

1. Talk about each photo. Ask the learner, "Show me the <u>application form</u>."

2. Ask the learner yes/no questions about the photos. Point to a photo and ask, "Is this the <u>owner</u>? The learner can answer *yes* or *no* or give a longer answer such as "Yes, that's <u>the owner</u>." or "No that's <u>the handyman</u>."

3. Point to photos and ask, "Who (or what) is this?" The learner answers, "The <u>owner</u>." or "The <u>owner of the restaurant</u>." or "<u>He's the owner of the restaurant</u>."

After You Watch

Note: In each unit the underlined words will change.

1. Ask the learner the questions to the left of the photos . The learner points to the correct photo and answers the question. For example, you say, "<u>Who is opening a restaurant</u>?" The learner points to Mr. Brashov's photo and gives a short or a long answer. For example: "<u>Mr. Brashov</u>." or "<u>Mr. Brashov is opening a restaurant</u>."

2. Ask the learner questions about the photos. Say, "Tell me about <u>Mr. Brashov</u>." The learner says, "<u>Mr. Brashov</u> is <u>opening a restaurant</u>. <u>His chef quit</u>. <u>He has to hire a chef and a waitress</u>."

Your New Language

1. Take turns speaking all of the conversations aloud. First you take the part of the first speaker in each activity and the learner takes the second part. Then the learner takes the part of the first speaker and you take the part of the second speaker.

2. Be sure the learner has opportunities to use the new language to talk about her personal life.

In Your Community

Note: In each unit, the underlined words will change.

1. Ask the questions in the *Worktext*. Listen to the learner's answers. Have the learner show you where she found the answers.

2. Collect additional <u>applications</u> for the learner to complete. Take turns asking and answering questions about the <u>application</u>.

Read and Write

Note: In each unit, the underlined words will change.

1. Ask the questions in the *Worktext*. Listen to the learner's answers. Have the learner show you where she found the answers.

2. Read the <u>diary</u> entry to the learner. Ask questions about it. Have the learner show you where she found the answers to your questions.

3. Have the learner read the <u>diary</u> to you and ask you questions about it. You answer and the learner finds your answers in the <u>diary</u>.

4. Have the learner read her journal writing to you and ask her questions about it.

What Do You Think?

1. Ask the questions in the *Worktext*. Listen to the learner's answers.

2. Ask the learner's opinions about topics or issues related to the story.

Culture Clip

1. Talk about the learner's responses in the *Worktext*.

2. Ask the learner questions about her opinions and experiences related to the cultural issue.

> **TIP** Have the learner tell you everything she knows about the characters from the *Worktexts* and the videos when you talk about the photos. If you haven't watched the videos, read the summaries at the back of the *Partner Guide*.

UNIT 1 "OPENING DAY"

Note: Use the sample questions in the **Unit Notes** or make up your own.

DON'T FORGET

to talk about the unit title

to review Worktext activities

to dictate sentences

to remind learners to write in their journals

Your New Language

Take turns asking and answering questions about personal information. Ask each other:

What's your name?
Can you spell that?
Where are you from?
Where were you born?

In Your Community

1. Take turns asking and answering questions about Katherine's job application. Ask:

    What is Katherine's address?
    When did Katherine fill out the application?
    Who is Katherine's reference?

2. Talk about the work you and the learner do or want to do. Take turns asking and answering these questions.

    Where do you work?
    What is your job?
    How did you get your job?
    Why do you like (or dislike) your job?
    What's your ideal job?

Read and Write

1. Talk about diaries. Take turns asking and answering these questions.

    Why do you think people write diaries?
    Why do you (or don't you) write a diary?
    How do you feel about reading another person's diary?

2. Katherine wrote in her diary about the people at Crossroads Café. Take turns asking and answering questions about people you and the learner work with.

Who do you like the best? Why?

Who do you like the least? Why?

Who is the most interesting person at work? Why?

What do you like (or dislike) about your boss?

What Do You Think?

Talk about what makes a good employee.

◆ Make a list of the characteristics of a good employee.

◆ Decide who will write the list.

◆ Take turns saying one characteristic until you have no more ideas. The writer should read the lists aloud to the other person.

◆ Put the items on the list in order of most important to least important.

Culture Clip

Talk about job interviews. Take turns asking and answering these questions.

What was your last job interview?

Who interviewed you?

How did you feel?

What did you wear?

What happened?

> **TIP** ► Look at pages 8–9 of this guide for more ideas about things to do with learners.

UNIT 2 "GROWING PAINS"

Your New Language

1. Talk about the last time you made introductions. Take turns asking and answering these questions.

Who did you introduce?

Where were you?

Why did you introduce this person?

What did you say?

2. Talk about introductions. Ask:

Who made introductions in the Worktext?

What did they say?

In Your Community

Talk about work-study permission forms with learners. Take turns asking and answering these questions.

Do you think work-study programs are a good idea? Why or Why not?

Do high schools have work-study programs in your native country?

Would you give your child permission to be in a work-study program?

Do you know anyone who does work study? Talk about this person.

Read and Write

Role-play a conversation about work-study programs.

◆ Decide who will have the conversation (student and high school counselor, parent and child, parent and high school counselor, student and employer, etc.)
◆ Write the conversation.
◆ Practice the conversation.

What Do You Think?

Talk about lying. Take turns asking and answering the following questions.

Why did Henry lie?
What would you do if you were Henry's parents?
What would you do if you were Mr. Brashov?
What do you think Henry learned?

Culture Clip

In the video, Henry wanted to be independent. Talk about children and independence. Take turns asking and answering these questions.

What decisions did your parents let you make for yourself when you were five?
What decisions did your parents let you make for yourself when you were 12?
What decisions did your parents let you make when you were 18?
When did your parents stop making decisions for you?
How was your family similar or different from other families in your culture?

TIP Don't do all the talking!

UNIT 3 "WORLDS APART"

Your New Language

1. Write the characters' names in this unit on a piece of paper.

◆ Brainstorm a list of things the characters want to do.
◆ Take turns asking each other, "What does <u>Mr. Brashov</u> want to do?" or "What does <u>Rosa</u> want?"
◆ Ask each other questions about all of the characters.

2. Look at a calendar with the learner. Take turns asking each other about tomorrow, the weekend, next week, and so on.

◆ Point to today and ask, "What do you want to do <u>today</u>?"
◆ Ask the learner to ask you the same question.

In Your Community

Get a telephone book and take turns asking each other to look up businesses. Say, "Find the number of a <u>florist</u>."

◆ When the learner finds a number, she dictates it to you.
◆ A variation is to dictate the phone number and the address.
◆ Look for the following businesses or make up your own list: florist, taxi cab, airline, school, bank, etc.

Read and Write

Interview each other about letter writing. Take turns asking and answering these questions.

When was the last time you wrote a letter?
Who did you write to?
Did you receive an answer to your letter?
Do you write to this person regularly?

What Do You Think?

1. Talk about Rosa's restaurant plans.

   ◆ Together make a list of everything Rosa wants to do in her restaurant.
   ◆ Take turns asking each other questions about her ideas. Ask:
      Do you think people will like Rosa's food?
      Do you think people will want to watch Rosa cook the food?
      Do you think people will want to eat foods from different countries?

2. Discuss why Rosa doesn't want to return to Mexico with Miguel. Ask each other:

   What do you think Rosa should do? Why?
   What do you think Miguel should do? Why?
   Do you know any people with the same problems as Rosa and Miguel? What happened?

Culture Clip

1. Ask the learner to think about when she came to the United States.

   Ask, "Why did you or your family come to the United States?"
   Ask, "How were your reasons similar to the reasons mentioned in the Culture Clip? How were your reasons different from the Culture Clip?"

2. Ask, "What do you wish you knew about the United States before you came?"

   ◆ Make a list of 5–7 tips for newcomers to the United States.
   ◆ Read the list and talk about the tips.
   ◆ Put the tips in order of importance from most important to least important.

3. Share your "life journeys" with each other.

   ◆ Make a list or draw pictures of 5–10 important events in your lives.
   ◆ Ask each other questions about the events.

UNIT 4 "WHO'S THE BOSS?"

Your New Language

1. Ask the learner to think about the last time she said, "I'm sorry." Ask:

   Who did you say, "I'm sorry" to?
   Why did you say, "I'm sorry"?

DON'T FORGET

to talk about the unit title

to review Worktext activities

to dictate sentences

to remind learners to write in their journals

2. Together decide what kind of apologies the learner made. Were they apologies for doing something wrong or were they just ways to "give bad news"?

3. Discuss how people make apologies in other countries. Ask, "How do people say 'I'm sorry' in your native country?"

4. Sometimes people give flowers or other small gifts to say, "I'm sorry." Talk about ways to say "I'm sorry." Ask, "What do you do when you want to say, 'I'm sorry'?"

In Your Community

1. Collect restaurant ads from your local newspapers or look at restaurant ads in your local telephone directory. Point to one ad at a time and take turns asking each other the following questions.

   What is the name of the restaurant?   *Where is it located?*
   What is the phone number?   *Are reservations accepted?*
   What time does the restaurant open?   *What time does it close?*
   What are the specials?   *Would you like to eat here?*

2. Interview each other about your favorite restaurants. Take turns asking each other questions like these:

   What is your favorite restaurant?   *Where is it?*
   How often do you eat there?   *How expensive is it?*
   *What do you like to eat at this
      restaurant?*

Read and Write

1. Collect several restaurant reviews from your local newspapers or magazines.

   ◆ Give the learner the reviews.
   ◆ Ask questions about the restaurants and have the learner circle or underline her answers. Then reverse. You look at the reviews and the learner asks you questions about it.

2. Talk about the learner's favorite neighborhood restaurant.

   ◆ Write some questions to ask the learner about the restaurant.
   ◆ Ask the learner the questions.
   ◆ Visit the restaurant together if you can.

What Do You Think?

Talk about why Jamal didn't want to tell his friends that he was a handyman. Ask:

Why do you think Jamal was embarrassed about his job?
Would you feel the same way? Why or why not?
What advice do you have for people who are embarrassed about their jobs?

Culture Clip

Today, many people change careers several times in their lifetimes. Talk about career changes. Ask each other questions like the following ones.

Do you want to change careers?

What do you want to do?

What education or training will you need?

How long will it take you to make this career change?

What is keeping you from making this change?

> **TIP** Remind the learner to complete the *Student Checklist* after each unit.

UNIT 5 "LOST AND FOUND"

Your New Language

1. Give simple directions to the learner. Use the following ones or make up your own. Say:

   Stand up.

   Walk over to the table.

   Pick up a book.

   Give me the book.

   Thank you.

   Sit down, please.

2. Ask the learner to think about other ways to ask people to do things.

   A. Give some examples if the learner is having difficulty thinking of things to say. Suggest:

      Why don't you close the door?

      Would you loan me a pen?

      Do you think you could hold this for me?

   B. Have the learner use these expressions to have you do things for her.

3. Ask the learner to give you simple directions to do something. Some ideas are: change a light bulb, tie your shoes, or make a bed.

   ◆ If the directions are not clear, say, "Please repeat that."

   ◆ Repeat the directions to the learner and say, "Is that correct?"

In Your Community

1. Do a safety tour of the place where you and your learner meet.

   ◆ Make a list of the safety precautions you see such as fire alarms, bars on windows, smoke detectors, etc.

   ◆ Compare the safety precautions to other places.

   ◆ Have the learner write a list of any new vocabulary and talk about the meanings and pronunciation of the words.

   ◆ Have the learner look up words in a bilingual dictionary if necessary.

2. Collect brochures, flyers, pamphlets, or newspaper articles about home security.
   ◆ Look at one piece of information at a time.
   ◆ Read the information silently.
   ◆ Take turns asking each other *yes/no* or *true/false* questions about the information.
   ◆ Conclude by talking about the new information you both have learned.

Read and Write

Talk about crimes that happened to the learner or someone she knows. Ask these questions:

What was the crime?
Who was involved?
What happened?

What Do You Think?

Talk about things people can do to be safe in their homes and communities.

◆ Have the learner make a list of 5–7 safety tips.
◆ Have the learner read the list aloud.
◆ Take turns asking questions about the tips. For example, ask, "Why should people leave their hall lights and/or their porch lights on at night?"

Culture Clip

Talk about crime in the United States and the learner's native country. Ask the following questions.

Which country has more crime—the United States or your native country?
What do you do to keep yourself or your family safe?
What could the United States do to reduce crime?

> **TIP** Ask the learner to talk about where she used English last week.

UNIT 6 "TIME IS MONEY"

Your New Language

1. Talk about problems you and the learner or your friends, relatives, or coworkers have.
   ◆ One person talks about a problem and the other person makes a suggestion about the problem.
   ◆ Each person should make three or more suggestions.

2. In the video, Emery Bradford made a lot of suggestions about ways to improve Crossroads Café.
   ◆ Make a list of Emery's suggestions.
   ◆ Take turns role-playing Emery making suggestions to Mr. Brashov.
   ◆ Try to use all of the expressions for making suggestions from the *Worktext*.

3. Take turns asking questions about people you and the learner make suggestions to. Ask, "Who do you make suggestions to? What suggestions do you make?"

In Your Community

1. Talk about schedules.

    ◆ Together make a list of as many schedules as you can think of.
    ◆ Put the schedules into categories such as transportation, work, school, etc.

2. Get a schedule from a school in your community. Most libraries have schedules and many schools send schedules to peoples' homes.

    ◆ Compare the schedule you get to the one on page 79 in the *Worktext*.
    ◆ Discuss the similarities and differences.
    ◆ Take turns asking and answering questions about the schedule.

3. Have the learner make a schedule of her daily activities. Ask her questions about what she does at specific times.

Read and Write

Discuss Emery Bradford by asking:

What do you like about Emery Bradford?
What do you dislike about him?
Do you know anyone similar to Emery? Describe this person.

> **TIP** ▶ Remind the learner to try to retell the story in English.

What Do You Think?

1. Have the learner think about things that are important to the characters in *Crossroads Café* and to herself. Start by asking questions about the characters. Then talk about personal opinions. Use the following ideas to get started.

    Which is more important to Mr. Brashov—making money or being happy?
    Which is more important to Emery Bradford—saving time or having friends?
    Which is more important to you—good health or money?

2. Discuss how the employees at Crossroads Café feel about the changes Emery made.

Culture Clip

Talk about how people in the United States and the learner's native country feel about time. Ask the learner if she agrees or disagrees with the following sentences. Have her explain her answers.

Time is money.
Time flies when you're having fun.
The early bird catches the worm.

UNIT 7 "FISH OUT OF WATER"

Your New Language

1. Take turns making sentences about things the employees at Crossroads Café did in the past and continue to do in the present. For example:

    ◆ Henry <u>has delivered</u> four lunches already today.
        (present perfect)

> **DON'T FORGET**
> to talk about the unit title
> to review Worktext activities
> to dictate sentences
> to remind learners to write in their journals

◆ Rosa <u>has taken</u> the bus to work everyday this week. (present perfect)

2. Take turns making sentences about things you and the learner did in the past and continue to do in the present. For example:

◆ We <u>have studied</u> English together for three months.

In Your Community

1. Ask the learner to think about special foods—foods she eats on holidays or at special events like weddings or birthdays.

◆ Ask, "In the video, when Victor and Nicolae were sick, their mother gave them chorba to eat. Did your mother give you anything special to eat when you were sick?"

◆ Take turns asking each other questions about special foods. Talk about the ingredients, utensils, or special preparations a person needs to make the special food.

2. Share favorite recipes. Take turns describing the foods and asking and answering questions about them.

Read and Write

1. Talk about sending and receiving postcards. Ask:

Where would you like to receive a postcard from?
Where would you like to send a postcard from?

2. Share any postcards you or the learner have received. Ask each other questions about the places on the postcards. Point to a postcard and ask:

Have you ever been to this place?
Would you like to go to this place? Why or why not?

3. Go to a store with the learner to buy a postcard. Have the learner decide to whom to send the card. Have the learner write the message, address the card, and mail it.

What Do You Think?

1. Talk about people the learner knows who are similar to the immigrants in the episode. Ask:

Who do you know who is similar to Victor?
Who do you know who is similar to Nicolae?
Who do you know who is similar to Rosa?
Who do you know who is similar to Jamal?

2. Have the learner retell Nicolae's dream. To help the learner, ask the following questions.

What happened first?
What happened second?
What happened third?
What happened next?

3. Talk about dreams. Ask each other the following questions.

Do you remember your dreams?

Describe a dream.

Have you ever had the same dream several times? What was it?

Do you believe dreams tell us something?

Culture Clip

Talk with the learner about when she first came to the United States. Ask:

Do you remember your first day in the United States? How did you feel?

How did you feel <u>one month</u> later? (Use your choice of time words for the underlined words in this question and the next one.)

How did you feel <u>one year</u> later?

How do you feel now?

> **TIP** Talk about how the learner's life is similar to or different from the characters in the videos.

UNIT 8 "FAMILY MATTERS"

Your New Language

1. Practice using different ways to offer to help people. Ask the learner to think about the last time she offered to help someone. Say, "What did you offer to do for someone? What did you say?"

2. Take turns offering to do something for each other. First you ask the learner, then the learner asks you. Try to use each of these expressions twice: "Would you like me to . . .?; I'll help you. . . ."

In Your Community

1. If you can, go to a public library or a school library with the learner. Use the on-line catalog to find information about a topic of interest to the learner or a book by the learner's favorite author. Some libraries have books and newspapers in different languages. Check to see if your library does.

2. Talk about computers. Take turns asking and answering these questions.

Do you have a computer at home? What kind is it?

Do you have plans to buy a computer?

Do you use a computer at work? How did you learn to use it?

Read and Write

1. In this video episode, Katherine made several bad decisions. She lied to her children about her job, and she asked her son David to babysit for his sister, Suzanne. Talk about Katherine's decisions. Ask:

Why did Katherine lie about her job? Would you have done the same thing? Explain.

Why did Katherine ask David to baby-sit for his sister? Would you have done the same thing? Explain.

What else could Katherine have done?

2. Look at the childcare ads in the local newspaper with the learner.

- ◆ Choose several ads.
- ◆ Take turns asking and answering questions about the ads.

What Do You Think?

Everyone has opinions about raising children. Talk about the problems parents have raising children today in the United States and in the learner's native country. Ask:

What are some of the problems parents have today in the United States?

What are some problems parents have in your native country?

Are these problems the same problems your parents had? Explain.

Where do you think it's easier to be a child—in the United States or in your native country? Explain.

Where do you think it's easier to be a parent—in the United States or in your native country? Explain.

Culture Clip

Talk about single parents. Take turns asking and answering these questions.

Do you know any single parents? Who are they? How old are their children?

What problems do you think single parents have in the United States?

Is there anything good about being a single parent? What?

> **TIP** Encourage the learner to try to speak English every day.

UNIT 9 "RUSH TO JUDGMENT"

Your New Language

1. Take turns describing each other.

- ◆ Look at each other for a minute or two without speaking.
- ◆ Each of you should make a list of words to describe each other.
- ◆ Include words to describe height, age, hair color, clothing, etc.
- ◆ Use the words to write 3–5 sentences about each other.
- ◆ Read the sentences aloud.

2. Have the learner describe a *Crossroads Café* character.

- ◆ Ask the learner to write 3–5 sentences about the character and read them aloud.
- ◆ Guess who the character is after the learner finishes reading her sentences.

In Your Community

1. Talk about reasons why people call the police. Ask, "Why do people call the police?"

- ◆ Make a list of reasons.
- ◆ Ask the learner if she has ever called the police for any of the reasons on the list.

2. Talk about calling the police to report a crime. Take turns asking each other the following questions.

> *Have you ever called the police? Why? What happened?*
>
> *Would you call the police to make a complaint about something or report a crime in your country? Why or why not?*
>
> *How are the police in your native country the same as police in the United States?*
>
> *How are the police in your native country different from the police in the United States?*

Read and Write

1. Use a telephone directory to read ads for lawyers.

- ◆ Ask "Why do people need lawyers?"
- ◆ Make a list of five reasons.
- ◆ Find an ad for a lawyer for each reason on your list.
- ◆ Choose one reason and one lawyer to call.
- ◆ Role-play a telephone call to a lawyer.

2. Use the telephone directory to find information about free or inexpensive legal services. Have the learner call the agency and ask questions about the legal services offered.

What Do You Think?

1. Take turns asking and answering questions about what happened to Jamal. Here are a few questions to get you started.

> *Why did the police pick up Jamal for questioning?*
>
> *Why didn't he have any identification?*
>
> *Why didn't the police believe Jamal's story?*
>
> *Do you think the police were rude to him? Why or why not?*

2. Take turns asking and answering questions about discrimination. Use the following questions.

> *What kind of discrimination have you experienced?*
>
> *What was the situation?*
>
> *What happened?*
>
> *How did you feel?*
>
> *What did you do?*
>
> *Would this have happened in your native country?*

Culture Clip

Talk about police officers' roles.

- ◆ Make a list of the things police officers do in your community. For example, in some communities police officers coach after-school sports. In other communities, police officers are assigned to work with youth groups. Some communities have Police Neighborhood Resource Centers.
- ◆ Read the list aloud.
- ◆ After each item, ask "Is this something you think the police should do?"

TIP Make arrangements to watch a video episode with the learner and talk about it as you watch.

UNIT 10 "LET THE BUYER BEWARE"

DON'T FORGET

to talk about the unit title

to review Worktext activities

to dictate sentences

to remind learners to write in their journals

Your New Language

1. Talk about compliments. Ask, "What kinds of compliments could the employees at Crossroads Café give each other?" Take turns role-playing the employees giving each other compliments. Here's an example to get you started.

   Partner: Rosa, you are wearing a very nice apron today.
   Learner: Thank you, Mr. Brashov. A friend gave it to me.

2. Compliment the learner on her glasses, hairstyle, jewelry, clothing, etc. Here are a few sample expressions. Use your own ideas for the underlined words.

   You are <u>friendly</u>.
   You are a very <u>cheerful person</u>.
   Your <u>earrings</u> are <u>beautiful</u>.
   Your <u>handwriting</u> is very <u>beautiful</u>.

3. Talk about how people feel when they receive compliments. Take turns asking and answering the following questions.

   How do you feel when someone compliments you?
   Are you comfortable or uncomfortable?
   What do you say when someone compliments you?
   Compare compliments in the United States to compliments in your native country.
   How are the compliments the same? How are they different?

In Your Community

1. Barbara was a con artist. She tricked Mr. Brashov to get his money. Talk about con artists. Ask the learner:

   Do you know anyone who was tricked by a con artist?
   What happened?

2. Discuss this expression: "You have to spend money to make money." Ask, "Do you agree or disagree with this sentence?" Explain your answer.

Read and Write

1. Have the learner reread the letter in the *Worktext*. Ask the learner to rewrite the letter in her own words without looking at the *Worktext*. After the learner has rewritten the letter, have her open the *Worktext* and compare the two letters.

2. Look for stories about con artists in the newspaper. Take turns reading the stories and asking and answering questions about them.

What Do You Think?

1. Talk about how people can avoid con artists and their tricks or scams.
   - Have the learner make a list of ways to avoid scams.
   - Read the list aloud and discuss it.
   - Put the ideas in order from most effective to least effective.
   - If possible, have the learner ask other people for their opinions about the list.

2. Talk about expressions related to money. Have the learner explain what the expression means. Ask, "Is there is a similar expression in your native language?" Here are a few expressions to discuss.

> *A fool and his money are soon parted.*
> *A sucker is born every minute.*
> *If it sounds too good to be true, it probably is.*

TIP Help the learner connect the video stories to her own life. Ask, "Has anything that happened in the video ever happened to you?"

Culture Clip

1. Take turns asking and answering questions about telemarketing.

> *What kinds of things do people try to sell you over the telephone?*
> *What do you do or say?*

2. Ask the learner to make a list during the next week or two of people who call trying to sell things. Talk about the calls and what the learner said to the callers.

UNIT 11 "NO VACANCY"

Your New Language

1. Use the following expressions from the *Worktext* to practice asking for clarification.

> *You mean . . .?*
> *What do you mean?*
> *What does that mean?*

2. Take turns role-playing these conversations or make up your own.

> *Tell your boss you don't understand his instructions.*
> *Tell your teacher you don't understand the homework.*
> *Tell your spouse you don't know what he is talking about.*
> *Tell a clerk in a store you don't understand why she can't give you the sale price on an item you want to buy.*

3. Ask, "What do you do or say in your native country when you don't understand?"
4. Take turns giving each other directions to do something such as sew on a button, wrap a present, or cash a check. Repeat each step of the instructions and use the expressions from #1.

In Your Community

1. Talk about completing rental applications. Ask these questions.

> *Have you ever filled out a rental application by yourself?*
> *Have you ever had help filling out a rental application?*
> *What did you do when you didn't understand a question on the form?*
> *Has anyone ever used you as a reference on a rental form?*
> *What does it mean to be a reference?*

2. Get a rental application form and practice completing it together.

Read and Write

1. Talk about experiences the learner has had with friends like Dorothy. Take turns asking and answering these questions.

   Were Dorothy and Katherine friends or friendly acquaintances? What's the difference?
   How did Katherine feel when she found out about Dorothy's prejudice?
   How did Dorothy feel when she found out Katherine helped Rosa prove discrimination?
   Would you have behaved like Katherine? Why or why not?

2. Have the learner retell what happened to Rosa.

What Do You Think?

Role-play with the learner one or more of the following situations.

Don and Patty are at home. They talk about what happened at the apartment.
Jamal tells his wife, Jihan, what he did to help Rosa.
Henry tells his parents about his video project.
Jess tells his wife, Carol, about what happened to Rosa.
Katherine tells her children what happened with Dorothy.

Culture Clip

Talk about discrimination.

1. Have the learner compare discrimination in the United States to discrimination in her native country.

2. Take turns asking and answering questions about discrimination for each of these categories: race, religion, gender (male/female), and age. Change the questions by changing the underlined words.

   Who do you think is discriminated against the most in the United States for race?

   Who do you think is discriminated against for race in your native country?

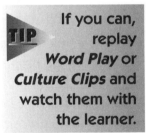

TIP If you can, replay *Word Play* or *Culture Clips* and watch them with the learner.

3. Share opinions about why people discriminate against each other.

UNIT 12 "TURNING POINTS"

Your New Language

1. Talk about ways to express possibilities. Ask "Do you know for sure what the weather will be tomorrow?" Nobody really knows for sure what the weather will be until it happens. At most, weather forecasters tell us what **might** happen.

   ◆ Talk about other things that **might** happen. Take turns asking and answering questions about what might happen.
   ◆ Here are some questions.

      What are you going to do tomorrow?
      What time are you going to go to sleep tonight?
      What are you going to do after dinner tonight?
      What are you going to watch on television tonight?
      What are you going to do this weekend?

2. Talk about what might happen in the next video.

In Your Community

Talk about crime in the learner's community. Have the learner make a list of the most recent crimes she has heard about. Ask her:

What is your community doing about crime?
What can you do to avoid being a victim of a crime?

Read and Write

1. Talk about the learner's personal reactions to a crime in the community. Look for a story in a local newspaper about a crime in the learner's neighborhood. Both of you read the story silently. Ask the learner these questions.

    What happened?
    Who was involved?
    When did the crime happen?
    What do you think will happen to the criminal?
    Could this crime have been prevented? Why or why not?

2. Have the learner write a letter to Henry about his news article.

> **TIP** A learner may not always want to talk about personal issues. That's OK!

What Do You Think?

Talk about Edward's problems with the gang. Have the learner make a list of advice for Edward.

Culture Clip

Talk about why people join gangs and the things we can do to eliminate them. Take turns asking and answering questions. Use these questions.

Do you know any people who belong to gangs?
Why do people join gangs?
What can parents do to keep their children from joining gangs?
What can schools do to keep kids from joining gangs?
What can communities do?

UNIT 13 "TRADING PLACES"

Your New Language

1. Make a list of things you and the learner can do. Ask the learner:

    What can you do?
    What do you know how to do?

2. Make another list of things you both can't do. Ask the learner:

    What can't you do?
    What don't you know how to do?

3. Have the learner talk about things the characters in the video *can* and *can't do* and *know how to do* and *don't know how to do*.

> **DON'T FORGET**
> *to talk about the unit title*
> *to review Worktext activities*
> *to dictate sentences*
> *to remind learners to write in their journals*

In Your Community

Have the learner practice reading the classified ads from local newspapers to find a job that interests her.

1. Say, "Look for jobs which interest you, and circle the three jobs that interest you the most."
2. Take turns asking each other questions about the jobs. Use the following questions as examples.

What is the job?   *Where is it?*
What are the qualifications?   *What are the hours?*
What is the pay?   *How do you apply?*

Read and Write

1. Talk about writing notes to say, "I'm sorry." Ask these questions.

   Why did Jess write a note instead of just saying, "I'm sorry"?
   How do you think Carol felt when she read Jess's note?
   How would you feel if someone wrote you a note to apologize?
   When would you write a note to say, "I'm sorry"?

2. Have the learner take the part of Carol and write a response to Jess's note.
3. Talk about which characters might write "I'm sorry" notes to each other.

   ◆ Make a list of the characters' names. Next to each name, write the name of a character to write a note to and a reason for the note.
   EXAMPLE: Edward to Mr. Brashov—vandalizing the café.
   ◆ Choose one character from the list and write a note.

What Do You Think?

In this video episode, the employees trade jobs and Carol and Jess have traded roles. Talk about trading jobs. Take turns asking and answering these questions.

Who would you like to trade jobs with? Why?
Who would you like to trade roles with? Why?

Culture Clip

1. Talk about the roles the learner has in her family. Make a list of the different jobs she has at home. Ask:

   Are any of the jobs unusual? Which ones?
   Are your jobs at home in the United States different from your jobs in your native country? Which ones? Why?

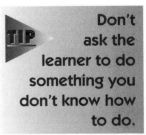

TIP Don't ask the learner to do something you don't know how to do.

2. Talk about the roles you have in your family. Compare them to the learner's roles. Talk about the similarities and differences.

UNIT 14 "LIFE GOES ON"

Your New Language

1. Take turns describing the characters in this video episode.

   ◆ Ask the learner to think about each character and tell everything she knows about that character—age, physical characteristics, personality, type of clothing worn, etc.

   ◆ While the learner is talking, write what she says.

   ◆ Read the learner's words or sentences aloud and ask if she wants to add anything.

   ◆ Here are a few examples to get started.

   > Rosa is <u>short</u>. She has very <u>curly</u> hair. She is too <u>tired</u> to cook at home. (The underlined words are adjectives; adjectives describe things.)

2. Take turns talking about what you had for breakfast, lunch, or dinner. Make a list. Describe the food on the list using the models from the *Worktext*.

In Your Community

1. Ask the learner to think about the medicines she takes when she is sick. Take turns asking and answering these questions.

   What do you take when you have a headache?
   What do you take when you have a stomachache?
   What do you take when you can't sleep?
   What do you take for a cold?

2. Ask the learner to think about where she buys medicine. Take turns asking and answering the following questions.

   Where do you buy over-the-counter medicine? Why do you buy it there?
   Where do you buy prescription medicine? Why do you buy it there?
   Do you have insurance for prescription drugs? How much do you have to pay?

Read and Write

Many people send get well cards to friends and family members who are sick. Talk about sending get well cards. Take turns asking and answering these questions.

Who do you send get well cards to?
What kind of cards do you send—humorous or serious?
Is it a custom to send get well cards in your native country?
If you sent cards in your native country, what kind of cards did you send?
What are some other ways to show you are concerned about someone?

What Do You Think

1. Talk about why Mr. Brashov wants to leave the hospital. Ask:

   What are Mr. Brashov's reasons for wanting to leave the hospital?
   Would you feel the same way? Why or why not?

2. Talk about which Crossroads Café employees would make the best boss. Ask:

> *Who would be the best boss?*
> *Why would this person be a better boss than anyone else?*

3. Take turns talking about luck. Ask:

> *Do you think Mr. Brashov is a lucky man? Why or why not?*
> *Do you think you are a lucky person? Why or why not?*

Culture Clip

1. Talk about hospitals in the United States. Take turns asking and asking these questions.

> *Have you ever been a patient in a hospital in the United States? What happened?*
> *Have you ever been a visitor in a hospital in the United States? Who did you visit?*
> *How did you feel? What did you think about the treatment?*
> *How are hospitals in the United States different from hospitals in your native country?*

2. Say, "A hospital is like a small city." Ask the learner to talk about why she thinks the statement is true or false. If the learner remembers the *Culture Clip* in the video, she can use examples from it.

> **TIP** After every unit, ask the learner to tell you what new things she learned.

UNIT 15 "BREAKING AWAY"

Your New Language

1. Take turns talking about the likes and dislikes of the characters in the video.

- ◆ Say a character's name. Ask the learner to talk about one thing the character *likes,* one thing the character *likes to do,* one thing the character *doesn't like,* and one thing the character *doesn't like to do.*
- ◆ Do the same thing for the other characters.

2. Take turns asking each other questions about things you *like, like to do, don't like,* and *don't like to do.*

3. Talk about other things the learner likes or dislikes. Ask, "What kind of <u>weather</u> do you like?" or "What's your favorite <u>sport</u>?" or "What kind of <u>weather</u> do you dislike?" or "What's your least favorite <u>food</u>?" (Substitute your own words for the underlined words.)

In Your Community

1. Talk about poster ads in the learner's community. Take turns asking and answering these questions.

> *Where do you see poster ads?*
> *What kinds of things are advertised?*
> *Do you pay attention to the poster ads? Which ones? Why?*

2. If the learner is interested, have her make her own poster for Crossroads Café or another restaurant or business she is interested in.

Read and Write

1. Collect newspaper or magazine articles about prejudice, intercultural events, or interracial issues to read and discuss.

2. Tell a story about prejudice from your personal experience. Ask the learner to take notes and ask you questions. Then ask the learner to share a personal story with you. You can take notes and ask the learner questions.

What Do You Think?

The characters in this video episode share a lot of opinions and make a lot of inferences. Remind the learner that inferences, assumptions, and conclusions are not always true. Use the following examples to show the difference between facts and inferences.

> **Fact:** Henry is Chinese.
> **Inference:** The Graysons don't like Henry because he is Chinese.

◆ Have the learner state 3–5 facts about the episode.

◆ Have the learner make 3–5 inferences about the episode. After each inference, talk about why the sentence is an inference, not a fact.

Culture Clip

TIP Review videos by asking learners to retell the stories.

Discuss intercultural, interfaith, or interracial relationships with the learner. Take turns asking and answering these questions.

If you were Henry and Sara's parents, would you have a problem with them dating? Why or why not?

Why are some people against intercultural, interfaith, or interracial relationships?

Do you know any people involved in intercultural, interfaith, or interracial marriages? What kinds of problems have they had? What are the benefits?

How would your parents or family feel if you were involved in an inter *relationship? Why?*

UNIT 16 "THE BOTTOM LINE"

Your New Language

1. Interview each other about yesterday.

◆ Ask the learner these questions. "What did you do yesterday? Who did you talk to? What did you talk about?"

◆ Have the learner write the answers to the questions you ask.

◆ Have the learners restate the answers to the questions you asked.

> EXAMPLE: **Question:** What did you do yesterday?
> **Answer:** I went shopping.
> **Restating the Answer:** I said I went shopping.
> I told you I went shopping.

[Note box:]
DON'T FORGET
to talk about the unit title
to review Worktext activities
to dictate sentences
to remind learners to write in their journals

2. Role-play characters from the video episode and take turns interviewing each other.

   - ◆ The interviewer asks a question, the *character* answers it, and the interviewer writes down the answer.
   - ◆ The interviewer asks a total of five questions and writes five answers.
   - ◆ The character reads the answers and restates them.

     EXAMPLE: **Question:** Why do you need to borrow money, Mr. Brashov?
     Answer: Mr. Brashov: Because I need to buy a new oven.
     Restating the Answer: You said you need to buy a new oven.

In Your Community

1. Discuss loans. Take turns asking and answering these questions.

   Have you ever filled out a loan application?
   What did you want to buy?
   Where did you apply for the loan?
   Did you have any problems completing the application?
   Do people apply for loans to buy things in your native country?
   Compare loans in the United States to loans in your native country. What's the same? What's different?

2. In the United States, it's important for people to establish credit. They do this by taking out a loan and paying it back on time or they apply for credit cards.

   - ◆ Talk about the advantages and disadvantages of buying things on credit.
   - ◆ Ask the learner, "What advice about buying things on credit do you have for newcomers?"
   - ◆ Have the learner make a list of tips about credit for newcomers.

3. Go to a local bank with the learner, if possible, and find out what kinds of loans they have. Get an application for a loan and fill it out together.

Read and Write

Ask the learner to fill out a loan or credit card application form. Review the form with her to make sure it is correct.

What Do You Think?

Talk about how Mr. Brashov could attract new customers to Crossroads Café.

- ◆ Ask the learner, "What suggestions do you have for Mr. Brashov?"
- ◆ Make a list of the suggestions.
- ◆ Decide together what Mr. Brashov should do first, second, third, and so on.

Culture Clip

Discuss senior citizens. Take turns asking and answering questions about seniors. Use these questions to start the discussion.

What advantages do senior citizens have?
What disadvantages do seniors have?
How are seniors treated in your native country?
Would you rather be a senior in the United States or in your native country? Explain why.

TIP ▶ Remind the learner to try the two and three star activities if she needs more challenge.

Unit 17 "United We Stand"

Your New Language

1. Many of the characters in this story complain about things or each other. Practice making complaints.

   ◆ Write the names of the characters in this video episode on a piece of paper.
   ◆ Take turns writing a complaint for each character on the list.
     EXAMPLE: **Jamal:** My tool box is missing.

2. Ask the learner to think about her own home or apartment.

   ◆ Ask, "What complaints do you have about your home? Who would you make the complaint to?"
   ◆ After the learner makes a complaint, guess who the learner is complaining to.
     EXAMPLE: **Learner:** Your room is a mess!
              Partner: You're talking to a teenager.

In Your Community

1. Talk about rental leases. Take turns asking and answering these questions.

   Have you ever signed a rental lease?
   When did you sign it?
   Did anyone translate the lease for you?
   Did you understand the lease?
   Have you had any problems with the lease?
   Are leases in your native country similar to leases in the Unites States? Explain.

2. Together, make a list of the most important things to include in a lease or a list of things people should look for in a lease. Put the items on the list in order of importance.

Read and Write

Talk about letters of complaint. Take turns asking and answering the following questions.

Have you ever written a letter of complaint?
Who did you write the letter to?
What did you complain about?
What happened?
When you don't write letters to complain, what do you do?

What Do You Think?

Talk about the steps people should follow when they make complaints to their landlords or to a company about a product.

◆ Decide together what the complaint is.
◆ Together make a list of the steps to take in making a complaint to a landlord.
◆ Put the steps in order.
◆ Read the steps to another person and ask for his opinion.

Culture Clip

Talk about tenant and landlord rights.

TIP ▶ Talk about the methods the learner used to guess the meanings of new words in this unit.

◆ Ask, "What things should tenants do?" and "What things should landlords do?"

◆ Together make a list of 5–7 things tenants should do.

◆ Make another list of 5–7 things landlords should do.

◆ Have the learner put the items on the lists in order.

◆ Ask the learner to share the lists with other people and ask for their opinions. The learner can report back to you at another session.

UNIT 18 "OPPORTUNITY KNOCKS"

Your New Language

1. Compare Jamal's job as a handyman at Crossroads Café with his new job as an engineer.

   ◆ Draw two columns on a piece of paper.
   ◆ Label one column HANDYMAN and the other column ENGINEER.
   ◆ Brainstorm as many things as possible that you know about each job.
   ◆ Use the information on the lists to make sentences comparing Jamal's jobs.
   EXAMPLE: Jamal's salary is higher at the construction company.

2. For more practice making comparisons, use the newspaper and find ads for cars, houses, or jobs. Choose two ads and take turns making sentences to compare them.
   EXAMPLE: Job #1 is closer to my home than job #2.

3. Take turns comparing life in the United States to life in the learner's native country. Some ideas about things to compare include: food, housing, people, clothing, sports, etc.

In Your Community

1. Take turns asking and answering questions about business cards. Use these questions or make up your own.

   Do you have business cards?
   Who do you give them to?
   Do people ever give you business cards?
   What do you do with the cards? Where do you keep them?
   Do people use business cards in your native country?

2. Collect some business cards. Take turns asking and answering questions about them. Try these questions.

   What's the name on the card?
   What's the business?
   What's the phone number?
   What's the FAX number?
   What's the email address?

3. If the learner doesn't have a business card, and is interested, ask her to design one for herself.

Read and Write

Most entry-level jobs do not require cover letters and resumés, so the learner may be unfamiliar with them. Take turns asking and answering questions about cover letters and resumés. Ask:

Do you have a resumé?

Have you ever written a cover letter?

Did you need a resumé or cover letter for your current job?

What kind of jobs require cover letters and resumés?

> **TIP** To review the video, have the learner retell the story in her own words.

What Do You Think?

Talk about why Rick Marshall hired Jamal. Take turns asking and answering these questions.

Why do you think Rick Marshall hired Jamal?

What kind of person did Rick think Jamal was?

In what ways did Jamal disappoint Rick?

What did Jamal learn from his experience at the construction company?

Culture Clip

If the learner works, talk about safety at work. If the learner doesn't work, talk about safety at home. Ask, "What kinds of safety clothing or equipment do you wear at work?" or "What kinds of safety rules do you follow at home?"

◆ Make a list of the safety items or rules.

◆ Take turns asking and answering these questions or make up your own. Ask, "Why do you wear _____?" (substitute the names of the safety items) or "Why do you _____ at home?"

UNIT 19 "THE PEOPLE'S CHOICE"

Your New Language

> **DON'T FORGET**
> to talk about the unit title
> to review Worktext activities
> to dictate sentences
> to remind learners to write in their journals

1. Talk about promises. Take turns asking and answering the following questions.

   Who do you usually make promises to?

   What kinds of promises do you make?

   Who usually makes promises to you?

   What kinds of promises do you make?

   How do you feel when you break a promise?

   How do you feel when people break promises to you?

2. Talk about the promises politicians make in the United States and in the learner's native country. Take turns asking and answering these questions.

   What kinds of promises do politicians make in the United States?

   What usually happens to their promises?

   What kinds of promises do politicians make in your native country?

   What usually happens to their promises?

3. Take turns making promises. After each promise, the other person guesses who the promise is to. Here are a few examples to get you started.

EXAMPLE #1: **Learner:** I promise not to fight with my brother anymore.
Partner: A child is making a promise to his parents.

EXAMPLE #2: **Learner:** I promise not to speed anymore.
Partner: A driver is making a promise to a police officer.

In Your Community

1. In the video, Jess had a problem with a $30,000 water bill. Talk about problems people have with utility bills. Take turns asking and answering these questions.

   What utilities do you pay?
   Have you ever had a problem with a utility bill? What happened?

2. Make a list of things people can do to keep their utility bills down.

   ◆ On a piece of paper, draw a column for each utility bill the learner pays.
   ◆ Write the name of the utility at the top of each column.
   ◆ Write the learner's ideas in each column.
   ◆ Ask the learner to share her ideas with another person.

Read and Write

1. Talk about what kinds of complaint letters get the best results—polite, threatening, angry, assertive, sad, etc.

   ◆ Ask the learner to think of a complaint.
   ◆ Together write two short letters of complaint using two different moods.
   ◆ Have the learner decide which letter is the most effective.

2. Have the learner write a thank-you letter to someone who helped her with a complaint.

What Do You Think?

Talk about making speeches. Ask:

◆ Think of a speech you liked. What did you like about it?
◆ Who are the best speech makers today? What makes them good speech makers?

Culture Clip

Talk about elected officials in your city and state. Take turns asking and answering the questions below. If the learner doesn't know the answers to any of the questions, talk about where she can find the answers. One place to suggest is the local library.

Who is the mayor of our city? How often is this person elected?
Who is the governor of our state?
What are our state's senators' names? How often are they elected?
What is the name of our representative to Congress? How often is this person elected?

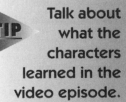

TIP Talk about what the characters learned in the video episode.

Your New Language

1. Take turns giving each other advice. Try to use **should** or **had better** in your sentences. Use the following situations or make up your own.

   ◆ You want to buy a used car.
   ◆ You are looking for a new apartment.
   ◆ You want to change jobs.

2. Role-play the following situation. Rosa is telling you about the favor Andrew Collins asked her to do for him. Give her advice. Use **should** and **had better** in your sentences.

In Your Community

1. Talk about movies. Take turns asking and answering these questions.

   Do you watch movies on television? Are the movies in English or your native language?

   Do you go to movie theaters to watch movies? Are the movies in English or your native language?

   What's the name of the theater you go to most often?

   Do you rent movies to watch at home?

   What's the name of the last movie you saw? Did you like it? Why or why not?

   What's your favorite kind of movie?

   Who's your favorite actor?

2. Find a movie schedule in the newspaper. Make plans to see a movie together.

Read and Write

In the *Worktext,* Rosa wrote a letter to her friend Carmen. Take turns reading the letter aloud. In the letter, Rosa says she is going to write Andrew a letter of apology.

   ◆ Ask, "What should Rosa say to Andrew when she writes a letter of apology to him?"
   ◆ Have the learner write Rosa's letter of apology to Andrew.

What Do You Think?

Talk about the characters in this video episode. Take turns asking and answering the following questions.

What do you think of Andrew Collins?

What's the best hair color for Rosa?

Should Rosa do any more translating jobs?

What made Stuart change?

Why should (or shouldn't) Katherine marry Bill?

Culture Clip

1. Talk about Mr. Shuster's problems with his son, Stuart.

    ◆ Have the learner retell the parts of the video that were about Mr. Shuster and Stuart.
    ◆ Make a list of words to describe Stuart.
    ◆ Ask, "What did Jamal and Henry do to change Stuart?"
    ◆ Ask, "How did Mr. Shuster feel about the new Stuart?"

2. Talk about raising children. Take turns asking and answering these questions.

    What things make it difficult to raise children?

    Is raising children easier or harder in the United States than in your native country? Why?

    What are some things your parents did that you think are good ideas?

    What are some things your parents did that you won't do?

    Who are the best parents you know? Why?

> **TIP** Ask the learner to tell you about people she knows who are like the characters in the video.

UNIT 21 "WALLS AND BRIDGES"

Your New Language

1. Talk about asking for and offering help.

    ◆ Each person makes a list of things that she needs to do.
    ◆ Take turns asking each other for help and offering to help each other.

2. Talk about the video episode. Take turns asking and answering the questions below.

    ◆ Who offered to help another person in the video? Who did this person help?
    ◆ What happened?
    ◆ How did the person who received the help feel?

In Your Community

Talk about report cards. Take turns asking and answering the following questions.

When you were a child, did your school send report cards home to parents?

How did you feel when your parents looked at your report card?

How are report cards in the United States similar to or different from report cards in your native country?

If you had to give yourself a report card for English, what would the grade be?

Read and Write

1. Talk about thank-you notes. Take turns asking and answering these questions.

    When was the last time you wrote a thank-you note? Who did you write to? What did you thank this person for?

    Did you buy a special card for your note or did you use stationery?

    Who do you usually write thank-you notes to?

    Do people write thank-you notes in your native country? Do they use special cards or do they use stationery?

2. In the video, Rosa wrote a thank-you note to Mr. Hernandez for meeting with her and Mrs. Scanlon.

  ◆ Have the learner take the part of María or her father and write a thank-you note to Rosa.
  ◆ Have the learner read her note aloud.

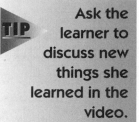

TIP   Ask the learner to discuss new things she learned in the video.

What Do You Think?

Talk about why César Hernandez changed his mind in the video.

◆ Ask, "Why did Mr. Hernandez change his mind?"
◆ Have the learner make a list of possible reasons.
◆ Have her chose the best reason and explain why.

Culture Clip

1. Talk about becoming a citizen. Take turns asking and answering the following.

> *Are you a citizen of the United States?*
> *If you are not a citizen, would you like to be one? Why or why not?*
> *What advantages do citizens have in the United States?*
> *What are the disadvantages to being a U.S. citizen?*

2. Have the learner call the INS (Immigration and Naturalization Service) to find out how to become a citizen.

3. Mr. Brashov had trouble studying for his citizenship test because he couldn't remember what he read. Talk about memory.

  ◆ What kind of a memory do you have—good or bad?
  ◆ What do you do to help yourself remember things?

UNIT 22 "HELPING HANDS"

Your New Language

1. Talk about asking for and giving permission to do things. Take turns asking and answering these questions.

> *What was something you asked permission to do recently?*
> *What did you say?*
> *Who did you ask? Did the person say yes or no?*
> *Where were you?*

2. Take turns asking for and giving permission. Use these expressions: "May I . . .?"; "Can I . . .?"; and "Do you mind if I . . .?" Substitute your own words for the underlined words.

> EXAMPLES: May I <u>look at your *Worktext*</u>?
> Can I <u>use your calculator</u>?
> Do you mind <u>if I open a window</u>?

3. Ask the learner to think about the video. Brainstorm a list of things the characters asked for permission to do. Read the list aloud.

> EXAMPLES: Frank said, "Do you mind if I take a look at the circuit box?"

DON'T FORGET

to talk about the unit title

to review Worktext activities

to dictate sentences

to remind learners to write in their journals

In Your Community

1. Talk about resumés. Take turns asking and answering these questions or make up your own.

   Do you have a resumé?
   Did anyone help you write your resumé?
   Did you need a resumé for your current job?
   If you don't have a resumé, are you interested in writing a resumé?

2. Companies that write resumés advertise in the yellow pages of the phone book or have ads in newspapers and magazines.

   ◆ Collect several ads for resumé services.
   ◆ Read and discuss several ads with the learner.
   ◆ Take turns asking and answering questions about the ads. Use these examples.
      What is the name of the company?
      What's the address?
      What's the telephone number?
      How much does it cost for a resumé?

3. If the learner wants more information about resumés, go with her to the local library to see what resources are available.

Read and Write

The airline lost Jamal's luggage when he took a trip to meet his wife.

◆ Take turns telling the story of what happened to Jamal.
◆ One person says a sentence and the other person writes the sentence.
◆ Continue taking turns saying and writing sentences until Jamal's story is told.
◆ Read the sentences aloud. Are they in the same order as the video?
◆ Rewatch the video, if you can, and check the order of the sentences about Jamal.

What Do You Think?

In the video, Jamal is angry with his wife, Jihan, and Katherine is suspicious of Frank. Ask:

Why is Jihan angry?
Why is Katherine suspicious?

Culture Clip

Talk about financial problems. Brainstorm a list of reasons why people have financial problems.

◆ Read the list aloud.
◆ Take turns giving solutions to the problems.

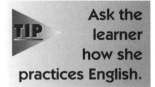

TIP ▶ Ask the learner how she practices English.

Your New Language

1. Take turns making, accepting, and rejecting invitations. Substitute your own words for the underlined words in the examples. Use the expressions on p. 132 of the *Worktext* to answer *yes* or *no*.

   EXAMPLE: I'd like to invite you to <u>go to a baseball game this weekend</u>.
   Would you like to <u>go shopping with me</u>?
   How about <u>taking an exercise class with me</u>?

2. Talk about invitations. Take turns asking and answering these questions.

   Who was the last person to invite you to do something?

   What was the invitation?

   What did the person say?

   Who was the last person you invited to do something?

   What was the invitation?

   What did the person say?

In Your Community

1. Talk about places the learner would like to visit. Take turns asking and answering the following questions.

   If you had the money, where would you like to go for a vacation?

   How would you travel to this place?

   How long would you stay in this place?

   Where would you stay?

   What would you do there?

   Who would go with you?

   How much money do you think you would spend?

2. Talk about places to go to get information about vacation places. Go with the learner to one of the places to get some information to read and discuss.

3. Make a list of local places people visit—parks, museums, zoos, amusement parks, etc. Choose one place to go to together.

Read and Write

1. Talk about birthdays. Take turns asking and answering these questions.

   Do people celebrate birthdays in your native country? If so, how are they celebrated?

   Have you been to a birthday party recently?

   Whose party was it? What did you do there?

   Did you give a gift? What was it?

   Did you give a card? What did it say?

2. Say, "Tell me about a birthday party you went to recently." If you don't know how to begin, use these questions. Then have the learner write about the party.

Whose party was it?
When was it?
Who was there?
What did people do?
Did people enjoy themselves?

What Do You Think?

1. Talk about vacations. Ask, "When was your last vacation? Describe it to me." As the learner talks, ask for more details.

2. Talk about the video. Take turns asking and answering the following questions.

   ◆ What did you think of the employees' plan to keep Mr. Brashov in town?

   ◆ Do you think it was a good idea or a bad idea? Explain.

   ◆ How would you feel if someone tricked you like the employees tricked Mr. Brashov?

Culture Clip

Talk about taxes. Brainstorm a list of taxes the learners pay. Read the list aloud. Ask:

Do you think you pay too many taxes? Why or why not?
What do you receive in return for your taxes?

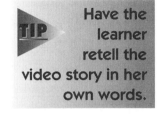

TIP Have the learner retell the video story in her own words.

UNIT 24 "ALL'S WELL THAT ENDS WELL"

Your New Language

1. Take turns asking and answering questions about the future using the following questions. Substitute your own words for the underlined words.

   What are you going to do <u>tomorrow</u>?
   What are you going to do <u>this weekend</u>?
   What will you do <u>at home tonight</u>?
   What will you do next <u>Saturday</u>?

2. Talk about Katherine and Bill's wedding.

   ◆ Brainstorm a list of things Katherine and Bill will do on their wedding day.

   ◆ Brainstorm a second list of things the wedding guests are going to do.

   ◆ Read both lists aloud.

   ◆ Decide if anything is missing from the lists and add those things.

In Your Community

Talk about invitations.

◆ Make plans for a party.
◆ Write the invitations.
◆ Use the future tense to talk about the plans.

Read and Write

1. Talk about thank-you notes. Take turns asking and answering these questions.

 ◆ Do you write thank-you notes for gifts? Explain why you do or don't write thank-you notes.

 ◆ Do you ever receive thank-you notes? Who sends them? Why?

2. Ask the learner to think about the last gift she received. Then ask her to write a thank-you note to that person. Have the learner read her note aloud.

What Do You Think?

Talk about all of the problems the characters in the video had while they were getting ready for Katherine and Bill's wedding.

 ◆ Brainstorm a list things that went wrong.

 ◆ Read the list aloud and take turns explaining how each problem was solved.

 ◆ Decide which problems could have been avoided and how.

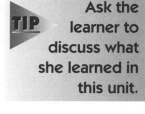

TIP ▶ Ask the learner to discuss what she learned in this unit.

Culture Clip

1. Take turns asking and answering questions about wedding customs in the United States and in the learner's native country.

 Ask, "What wedding customs did you see in the video?" Make a list.

 Ask, "Are any wedding customs in your native country the same? What are they?" Make another list.

 Ask, "What wedding customs are different in your native country?" Make another list.

2. Read all of the lists aloud. Ask, "Do you want to add anything?"

UNIT 25 "COMINGS AND GOINGS"

Your New Language

1. Talk about future plans and possibilities. Take turns asking and answering these questions or make up your own. Use *I'm going to . . .* and *I might . . .* in the sentences. Substitute your own words for the underlined words.

 What things are you sure you're going to do <u>today</u>? (Things you are sure will happen.)

 What are some things you might do <u>today</u>? (Things that may happen, but you're not sure about.)

2. Talk about the characters in the video.

 ◆ Draw two columns on a piece of paper.

 ◆ Write GOING TO HAPPEN at the top of one column and MIGHT HAPPEN at the top of the other column.

 ◆ Ask, "What is going to happen to <u>Katherine</u>? What might happen to <u>Katherine</u>?" (Substitute the other characters' names for Katherine's name.)

 ◆ Ask the learner to say one or two things that are going to happen and might happen for each character.

 ◆ Write the learner's responses in the proper columns.

 ◆ Read the columns aloud. Explain why you agree or disagree with the learner.

DON'T FORGET

to talk about the unit title

to review Worktext activities

to dictate sentences

to remind learners to write in their journals

In Your Community

1. Ask, "Do you have an application that you filled out?" Look at it together taking turns to ask and answer questions about it.

2. Talk about the schools in the learner's community. Take turns asking and answering questions.

   What schools are in your community?

   What kind of schools are they?

   Do you know any people who go to those schools? Who?

   Have you ever been to any of those schools? Which? Why?

Read and Write

Take turns reading aloud Katherine's *friendly note* to Mr. Brashov. Ask, "How would Mr. Brashov answer the note?" Ask the learner to write a note from Mr. Brashov and read it to you.

What Do You Think?

Talk about the characters in the video. Take turns asking and answering the following questions.

Which character is most like you? Why?

Why does Jamal want to return to Egypt?

Have you ever wanted to return to your native country? Why or why not?

Why shouldn't Henry drop out of school? Have you ever thought about dropping out of school? Why or why not?

Jess told Victor to slow down and leave time for important things. Do you leave time for important things? What are some of your important things?

Culture Clip

Talk about why some people leave the United States and return to their native countries. Think about the **Culture Clip** part of the video and the people you know.

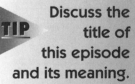
TIP Discuss the title of this episode and its meaning.

- Draw two columns on a piece of paper.
- Label one column REASONS TO STAY in the United States and label the other column REASONS TO RETURN HOME.
- Read the reasons aloud and discuss each one.

UNIT 26 "WINDS OF CHANGE"

Your New Language

1. Talk about things you *have to do* or *must do*. Substitute your own words for the underlined words. Ask, "What are some things you have to do <u>today</u>?"

2. Talk about things the characters in the video *have to do* or *must do*.

   - Draw a chart on a piece of paper with one column for each character's name.
   - Take turns saying one thing each character *has to do* or *must do*. Use both expressions in the sentences.
   - Try to say two or three things for each character.
   - Read the lists aloud.

In Your Community

1. Talk about reading maps. Ask the learner to draw a map of her neighborhood. Ask questions about places on the map.

2. Ask the learner to give directions from her home to the learning place.

Read and Write

1. Read aloud Mr. Brashov's good-bye letter on page 178. Then ask:

   Do you agree with Mr. Brashov's letter?
   Would you make any changes?
   What would you say differently?
   What other advice would you give?

2. Talk about good-bye letters. Ask:

   Have you ever written a good-bye letter?
   Who did you write to?
   Why did you write instead of just telling that person good-bye?

3. Have the learner choose a character from the video and write a good-bye letter from that person to another character in the video. Ask the learner to read aloud her good-bye letter.

What Do You Think?

Talk about the characters in the video. Take turns asking and answering these questions.

Should Carol keep the chess set? Why or why not?
Should Mr. Brashov accept the cruise tickets from Carol? Why or why not?
Should Mr. Brashov offer to pay for the tickets? Why or why not?
Will Mr. Brashov enjoy the cruise? Why or why not?
Will Rosa be a good manager of the café? Why or why not?
Will Henry graduate from college? Why or why not?
Will Katherine be happy with Bill?
Will Jamal be happy in Egypt?

Culture Clip

Talk about goals. Take turns asking and answering the following questions or make up your own.

What were your goals when you came to the United States?
What are your goals now?
What are your goals for learning English?

> **TIP** ▶ Discuss what the learner liked about learning English with *Crossroads Café*.

Victor Brashov is from Romania. He came to the United States 40 years ago. Now he is in his sixties and he is starting a new business. He is opening a restaurant.

It is a few days before the restaurant opens. Nothing is ready, but there are many people in the restaurant. Most of the people are workers. They are trying to get the restaurant ready to open.

One worker is Jamal. He is a handyman and a friend of Mr. Brashov. Jamal is from Egypt. He has a degree in engineering. He tries to fix Mr. Brashov's broken stove. This is a new kind of work for Jamal.

Another worker is a sign painter. He wants to paint the name of the restaurant on the sign. But Mr. Brashov does not have a name for his restaurant. This is just one of his many problems.

The chef is angry because the stove doesn't work. He quits. Now Mr. Brashov doesn't have a cook for his restaurant. He doesn't have any waiters or waitresses either.

Mr. Brashov puts an ad in the newspaper for waiters and waitresses. Several people come to apply for the jobs. Mr. Brashov doesn't like any of them.

Katherine Blake comes in. She was a waitress many years ago. She stayed home to take care of her children for ten years. Mr. Brashov likes Katherine, and he gives her a job.

Another woman comes to the restaurant. Her name is Rosa Rivera. She is from Mexico. Rosa also wants to be a waitress. But she can cook, so Mr. Brashov hires her to be the chef.

Now Mr. Brashov has employees. He can open his restaurant. But on opening day, the restaurant still does not have a name.

A teenager comes into the restaurant. His name is Henry. He is 17 years old and he is in high school. Today, there is no school. He needs directions to the post office.

Someone calls the restaurant and wants some food delivered. It is the first order. Mr. Brashov asks Henry to deliver the food.

Another person comes into the restaurant. He wants some coffee. His name is Jess Washington. Jess is retired. He worked for the post office. Jess likes to play chess. He plays with Jamal.

The sign painter is still in the restaurant. He wants to know the name of the restaurant. Everyone suggests names. Mr. Brashov does not like any of the names. Then Jess has an idea. He thinks Crossroads Café is a good name. Mr. Brashov likes it. Finally, the restaurant has a name!

UNIT 2   GROWING PAINS

Two unexpected visitors surprise the employees at Crossroads Café. The first unexpected visitor is Margaret Reilly. She's an inspector with the Department of Health and Safety. She is looking for health and safety problems in the café.

The second unexpected visitor is Henry's uncle. He and his friend are at Crossroads Café for a take-out order. Henry doesn't want his uncle to see him because his parents don't know about his job.

Henry tries to hide from his uncle. Rosa asks Henry, "What's going on?" Henry tells her, "My parents don't know I am working here." Rosa wants Henry to tell Mr. Brashov about this, but Henry is afraid to tell him.

Ms. Reilly, the inspector, makes the employees nervous. She walks around and writes on a clipboard. She is not very friendly. She wants to inspect everything: Mr. Brashov's office, the bathrooms, and the kitchen. She has a lot of questions. She wants someone to show her around the café and answer questions. Jamal shows her around the café.

Henry tells Mr. Brashov, "I have something important to talk to you about." But Mr. Brashov does not understand. He tells Henry not to worry. He is doing a good job.

When Henry gets home, there is a birthday party at his house. It is his brother's 13th birthday. Henry's uncle comes to the party. Mr. and Mrs. Chang find out about Henry's job. They are very angry. Henry's parents want him to quit his job at Crossroads Café. They don't think Henry can do schoolwork, practice the violin, and work.

At Crossroads Café, Jamal helps Ms. Reilly. He shows her around the restaurant and answers her questions. Ms. Reilly finds some toxic chemicals. She says they are dangerous to have around food. She gives Mr. Brashov some forms to fill out. Mr. Brashov is worried about the inspection.

Mr. and Mrs. Chang come to Crossroads Café. Mr. Brashov finally learns about Henry's problem. Now he finds out about Henry's big lie. Henry's parents did not give him permission to work. They did not sign the work permission form from Henry's school. Someone else signed it! Now Mr. Brashov is angry, too.

Ms. Reilly is still in the café. She talks to Katherine and Rosa. Katherine has a headache after she talks to Ms. Reilly. But Rosa is happy to talk to Ms. Reilly. She loves to show people her kitchen. She gets along very well with Ms. Reilly.

Then everyone hears a scream. It's Ms. Reilly. Henry's violin case was in the kitchen. Ms. Reilly fell over it. She complains to Mr. Brashov. Now Mr. Brashov is really worried about the inspection.

Mr. and Mrs. Chang are surprised to see Henry's violin case. They are happy because Henry is practicing his violin. They tell him, "If you keep up with your school work and violin lessons, you can keep your job." They will decide in a few weeks.

Two weeks pass. Mr. Brashov is opening the mail. It's good news. First there is a report from Ms. Reilly. Crossroads Café passed the inspection. There is also a letter from Mr. and Mrs. Chang. They signed Henry's work form. He can keep his job!

WORLDS APART

Lunch hour is almost over at Crossroads Café. Two women, Mrs. Gilroy and her friend want to order lunch. Mrs. Gilroy suggests the special, Monterey Chicken.

The two women see Mr. Brashov. Mr. Brashov looks very tired. He is not sleeping well at night. When he comes to work, he is tired and he forgets things.

Rosa enters the café with her friend Miguel. She introduces him to Mr. Brashov and the other employees. Miguel is from Rosa's hometown, Puebla, Mexico. Miguel is an architect, and he is on his way to a conference.

Rosa takes Miguel to her apartment. She wants to introduce Miguel to her roommate, Carrie. But Carrie is not home. Miguel gives Rosa a necklace. The necklace belonged to his mother and his grandmother.

Miguel wants to marry Rosa. He wants her to return to Mexico to live. Rosa tells Miguel about her dreams. She is taking business classes because she wants to have her own restaurant someday. He says, "You can open a restaurant in Puebla, Rosa. I will help you."

When Miguel leaves her apartment, Rosa cannot sleep. She stays up late and thinks about her restaurant. She draws plans for the building, and she thinks about the menu.

The next day, Rosa tells Miguel about her ideas for her restaurant. Rosa wants to have the kitchen in the middle of the restaurant so people can watch her cook. She also wants to have international food on the menu. Miguel says, "You forget, Rosita. This is Puebla, Mexico. The people in Mexico will not come to your restaurant." This makes Rosa very sad.

At the café, Mr. Brashov's brother Nicolae calls. He will send Mr. Brashov something to help him sleep. It is almost lunch time, but Mr. Brashov leaves the café. He goes to the bank to sign loan papers.

Then the phone rings. It is for Katherine. Her daughter was hurt at school. Katherine must go to the hospital. When Katherine leaves, there is no waitress.

A group of women enter the café. They made a lunch reservation with Mr. Brashov, but he forgot to tell Rosa. Because Mr. Brashov and Katherine are not at the café, Rosa must do their jobs. She greets the customers and takes their food orders. Henry helps her.

The women want to eat Rosa's special chicken recipe, but it's not on the menu today. Rosa likes to try out new recipes. She persuades them to try Chicken San Joaquin, and they love it.

Rosa does not want to go back to Mexico. She wants to live in the United States. The U.S. is her home now. Miguel does not understand this. Rosa decides not to marry Miguel.

The next day a package comes from Nicolae in Romania. He knows why Victor cannot sleep, so he sends Victor a special pillow. The pillow belonged to Mr. Brashov when he was a boy.

Then Victor remembers. It is his 40th wedding anniversary, and he misses his dead wife. Now, he can sleep again.

UNIT 4   WHO'S THE BOSS?

Jamal was an engineer in Egypt. He designed bridges and highways. Now he is a handyman at Crossroads Café. Jamal is trying to fix the café's alarm system, but he is having a few problems.

Mr. Brashov is waiting for a phone call from the *Restaurant News.* He wants the newspaper to write about Crossroads Café so it will have more business.

Jamal asks to go home early. He and his wife, Jihan, are going out in the evening. They're going to a special reception for an important man from Egypt. The man used to be Jamal's boss. Mr. Brashov says, "Of course you can leave early for such a special occasion."

Jess is in the café. He doesn't hear Katherine when she talks to him. Mr. Brashov decides to talk to Jess about his hearing problem. But Jess gets angry and leaves the café.

That night at the reception, Jamal meets some old friends from Egypt. His friends talk about their jobs, and they want to know about Jamal's job. Jamal says, "I'm in the restaurant business now." He doesn't say, " I am a handyman." Jamal is embarrassed because he doesn't have a professional job anymore.

The next day, someone from the *Restaurant News* calls Crossroads Café. A reporter is coming to interview Mr. Brashov. But he doesn't know when the reporter will come. Mr. Brashov decides to go to the bank.

While Mr. Brashov is at the bank, Jamal's friends from Egypt come to the café. They want to surprise Jamal. But he is not happy to see his friends because they think he's the boss.

Jamal decides to act like the boss. That makes Katherine and Rosa angry. They don't know about Jamal's friends in the café. Finally, Jamal tells Rosa and Katherine his problem. They decide to help Jamal, and they pretend he is the boss.

But then Mr. Brashov comes back from the bank. He asks Jamal, "How is the burglar alarm coming?" Jamal tells Mr. Brashov to fix it right away. Mr. Brashov is very surprised. He asks, "Who is the handyman around here?" And Jamal says, "You are?"

Then Katherine takes Mr. Brashov into the kitchen. She tells him about Jamal's problem. Now Mr. Brashov also pretends Jamal is the boss. He apologizes to him.

Jess comes into the café. His ears were cleaned and now he can hear. But he is confused because Mr. Brashov calls Jamal "boss."

Henry comes to work. He doesn't know Jamal is the "boss." He is confused, too. Then, a man in the café stands up. He is from the *Restaurant News,* and he wants to interview the owner. Jamal has to tell his friends the truth about his job.

Jamal didn't need to lie to his friends. They admire Jamal because he left everything in Egypt to come to the United States. They don't care if Jamal is a handyman or a restaurant owner. They are his friends.

The next day Jess brings a newspaper into the café. There is an article about Crossroads Café. The title is "Who's the Boss?".

UNIT 5   LOST AND FOUND

Katherine lost her keys. The other employees help her look for them. Finally, Mr. Brashov finds the keys. They were next to the coffee machine.

A police officer is at Carol and Jess Washington's house. They are reporting a burglary. Someone robbed their house. It is a mess. The burglar stole an old TV, a VCR, and a toaster oven. The burglar also broke Jess's wooden airplane.

Jess comes into Crossroads Café. Several people are eating lunch. A woman is asking questions about the fish. Then the door to the café opens. Three young boys come running in the door. They are shouting and throwing a football. When Mr. Brashov tells them to stop, they are rude to him. The customers in the café do not like this, and they walk out.

One of the young boys is Katherine's son, David. Katherine is very angry. Katherine sees David's watch. "Where did you get it?" she asks. David says, "I found it at school." Katherine knows this is a lie. The counselor at David's school called her. David did not go to school this week.

The boys leave the café. Katherine argues with David. A few minutes later, David runs out of the café. Katherine is very worried about David. It is hard for Katherine to be both a mother and a father to David.

A salesperson from "A to Z Security" is at the Washington's house. He is trying to sell Jess and Carol a security system. It is very expensive, so Jess and Carol do not buy it.

David is at Crossroads Café again. This time he is doing homework in the utility room. He is not happy to be there. He throws his books and papers on the floor. Then he picks up a hammer and hits some wood.

Jess comes into the room. He sees David with the hammer. "Does that hammer belong to you?" Jess asks David. David says to Jess, "You sound like a cop."

Jess and David talk. They talk about their fathers. When Jess was 10 years old, his father went away. He left Jess a note and a wooden airplane. The burglar broke it.

David's parents are divorced. He used to build things with his father. Now he never sees him. David's feelings are very hurt.

Jess worries about safety all of the time. He reads newspaper stories about crime. He asks Jamal to hook up an alarm system. It doesn't work. Jess doesn't want Carol to go out alone at night. Carol thinks Jess worries too much. She invites people in the neighborhood to her house to talk about safety. Many people come to the meeting.

Katherine is waiting for David to come to the café after school. He is late, and she is not happy. Finally, David comes. He was in the wood shop at school. He has a friend with a broken airplane, and David wants to fix it. Jess is the friend.

The employees think of other things for David to make. They suggest a coat rack and a sign for Rosa's specials. But Rosa has the best idea. She suggests a key holder for Katherine.

Mr. Brashov is sitting at a table in the café. He is not working in his office because Jamal is fixing the air conditioner. Mr. Brashov is unhappy. He likes owning a business, but he hates the paperwork.

Henry is late for work and everyone is waiting for him. Katherine has to pick up her children from school. Rosa has to go to the library before her business class. Mr. Brashov tells them to go. Finally, Henry comes. He was buying tickets for a rock concert.

Jess has a suggestion for Mr. Brashov. His son has a friend from school, Emery Bradford. Emery can help organize Mr. Brashov's paperwork. Jess gives Emery's business card to Mr. Brashov and tells him to call Emery. Mr. Brashov is not interested.

The air conditioner comes on. Unfortunately, it blows Mr. Brashov's paperwork on the floor. Then he takes Emery Bradford's business card from Jess.

Rosa is at her business management class. The teacher has a special project for the class. Rosa and Armando, another student, will be managers of a mail room. They have to organize the other students so they can wrap a package to send.

Armando's team works well together. He encourages them to do a good job. Rosa's team does not work well together. She tells them what to do and tries to make them work faster. Rosa takes over. Her team did not do well, and she feels like a failure.

Emery is at Crossroads Café. He organizes Mr. Brashov's paperwork and helps him make a schedule for paying bills. He walks around with a clipboard and timer. He watches the employees and makes notes. Emery looks for ways to save time. He tells Mr. Brashov, "Time is money."

Emery makes many changes at Crossroads Café. The employees work faster and wear uniforms now. Mr. Brashov is wearing a white shirt and bow tie.

Emery announces a contest. Mr. Brashov will give $100 to the most efficient employee. But Mr. Brashov is not happy. He likes to talk to the customers. Emery does not like this. If Mr. Brashov talks to the customers, they sit at the tables too long. Emery wants customers to eat quickly and leave, so there are tables for more customers.

Finally Emery announces the winner of the contest. Katherine hopes to be the winner. But she is not. It is Rosa. Then Rosa surprises everyone. She does not accept the prize. She says, "The award does not belong just to me. It belongs to all of us." Rosa understands teamwork now.

Mr. Brashov disagrees. He thinks Emery should win the award. He gives Emery the trophy and the check and says good-bye. He takes off his tie and throws it in the air.

Several days later, everything is back to normal at Crossroads Café. Jamal makes an announcement. The air conditioner is fixed. He turns it on, and it blows Mr. Brashov's papers all over the room.

It is almost closing time at Crossroads Café. Everyone is waiting for Mr. Brashov and his brother Nicolae. Nicolae is coming from Romania. He was the manager of a tourist hotel on the Black Sea. Now he will be Mr. Brashov's new partner.

The door opens and everyone welcomes Nicolae. He is younger and thinner than Mr. Brashov. He also speaks English very well.

Nicolae recognizes the employees at Crossroads Café because Victor sent him pictures. But Nicolae doesn't know Jess. When Victor introduces Jess to Nicolae, Victor says, "Meet Crossroads Café's best customer."

When everyone leaves, Victor and Nicolae are alone. They talk and eat a snack. Nicolae wants to speak Romanian. Victor doesn't. His brother does not understand why Victor isn't interested in Romania.

The café is open. Nicolae is trying to learn about the business. First he drops plates when he serves customers. Then he uses a cart. He helps Jamal. He teaches Rosa a new recipe. He figures out how to save money, and he plays chess with Jess. He even wants to help Henry with deliveries.

Nicolae says, "We used to ride bicycles all the time. Why stop now?" Victor taught him to ride a bicycle when he was a boy. He wants to ride a bicycle again with his brother. Victor has no time. Work at the café comes first.

Victor has the flu. Nicolae runs the restaurant for him. He changes the menu, redecorates, and hires Romanian musicians. Crossroads Café looks like a Romanian restaurant.

When Victor returns to the café, he is very angry. He tells the musicians to go. He argues with Nicolae. Nicolae is angry, too. He says to Victor, "You are ashamed of our customs, our language." Nicolae leaves the café.

Nicolae is at a mall. He is buying something, and he sees one of the Romanian musicians. Nicolae tries to follow him, but there are too many people.

Nicolae is walking in the mall. He sees the musician again. Then Nicolae loses his wallet. He takes candy from a little girl, but he doesn't pay for it. The little girl tells a police officer. Nicolae sees them talking. He looks for his wallet, but he cannot find it. He gives the candy to the police officer and runs away.

Nicolae is on the street again. A woman asks him for money and he gives her everything in his pocket. Then Nicolae hears some music. He follows the music and climbs some stairs. He is in a Romanian cabaret. Romanian music is playing. Everyone from Crossroads Café is there, but they do not see Nicolae or speak to him. They ignore him. Finally a man speaks to Nicolae in Romanian. Nicolae asks, "Where am I?" The man says, "You are home."

Mr. Brashov is very sad. Nicolae is at the airport. He is going back to Romania. Nicolae gave Victor a package before he left. Mr. Brashov opens it. It is a beautiful music box.

A man comes into the café. He found Nicolae's wallet. Victor calls the airport to tell Nicolae. He also says, "I know you need to go. I want to visit you soon. We can ride bicycles, too."

Katherine is very tired and worried. Her son, David, doesn't like to do school work. David will have a birthday soon; he will be 14 years old.

Henry is happy and full of energy. He is dating Sara, a girl from school. Sara is in Henry's social studies class.

Everyone at Crossroads Café is worried about Katherine. They want to help her, but she won't talk about her problems.

Katherine asks Jamal about computers. She shows him an ad for a computer in a catalogue. This computer is cheaper than the other computers. Jamal says, "It's a close out." The computer is cheap because it is not a new model.

Katherine comes home from work. Her children are fighting. David wants to watch a football game. Suzanne, David's eight-year-old sister, doesn't. Katherine tells them to take turns choosing TV programs.

David is not happy. He has to babysit his sister after school. He can't be with his friends. He asks his mother, "Why do you have to work this second job anyway?"

Katherine is working two jobs because she wants to buy David a computer for his birthday. It's a surprise. Katherine can't tell David and Suzanne the truth about her second job.

Sara comes to Crossroads Café to see Henry. She tells him about a formal dance at school.

Rosa asks Henry about the school dance. Henry is not going to the dance because he doesn't know how to dance. Rosa offers to teach him. Sara comes into the café and sees Henry dancing with Rosa. Sara is jealous and walks out.

Rosa asks Katherine to go shopping after work. Katherine says no. She has no time. Rosa's feelings are hurt. Later that evening, Rosa goes to Katherine's apartment. Suzanne is alone. She tells Rosa about Katherine's second job.

Suzanne is drawing a picture. Rosa looks at it. Suzanne drew two unhappy children. Then Katherine comes home. She is surprised and a little angry to see Rosa. Rosa shows Suzanne's drawing to Katherine. She feels very sad when she sees the drawing. Then David comes home and argues with his mother.

The next day at work, Katherine is upset. David would not talk to her in the morning. She calls home after school, but the children are not there.

Finally Katherine tells Mr. Brashov and the other employees about her second job. While she is talking to them, the door to the café opens. It is David and Suzanne. David fixed Jess's airplane. He is bringing it to Jess.

Katherine doesn't see David and Suzanne, but they hear her. They do not want money. They want to be with their mother. They love her. Katherine decides to celebrate David's birthday early. She will take her children to the lake for a long weekend.

Then Sara comes to the café to talk to Henry. He explains about Rosa. He says, "I can't dance and Rosa was teaching me." Henry asks Sara to go to the school dance.

Two police detectives are in Crossroads Café. Mr. Brashov met them last week. Henry comes into the café with his grandparents. Mr. Brashov introduces Henry to the police officers. Henry's grandparents are afraid of the police. The police were not very nice to them in China. Henry doesn't think the police are very nice in the U.S., but Mr. Brashov disagrees with him.

Henry's grandparents don't speak much English. They are going to take the bus to the senior citizens' center for flu shots. Henry gives them a map and takes them to a bus stop.

Jamal is late for work. He is walking down the street with his toolbox. The toolbox opens and the tools fall out. Two policemen are watching from a car. When they see Jamal's tools, they get out of their car. They ask Jamal for identification. He does not have his wallet or his driver's license.

The police ask Jamal, "Where were you last night around 11:30?" Jamal was home with his wife and sick daughter. The police want to check Jamal's story with his wife. But Jamal's wife is out of town on business. The police do not like Jamal's answers to their questions. They decide to take him to the police station.

Jamal calls Mr. Brashov. Jamal is very upset and Mr. Brashov cannot understand him. Mr. Brashov tells Jess and Katherine, "It's something about burglaries." Jess saw an article in the newspaper about some recent burglaries. The description of the burglar sounds like Jamal.

Mr. Brashov goes to the police station. He waits a long time to see Jamal. Nobody answers Mr. Brashov's questions.

While Jamal and Mr. Brashov are at the police station, Henry comes back to the café. His grandparents are lost. They did not go to the senior citizens' center. Jess offers to help Henry look for his grandparents.

Jess and Henry cannot find the two old people, so they return to the café. Then Henry's mother comes in. She wants to take her parents home. Henry doesn't want to tell his mother the truth. Jess helps Henry. He tells Henry's mother, "I'll drive your parents home when they come back to the café."

At the police station, one of the detectives recognizes Mr. Brashov. Mr. Brashov identifies Jamal, and he gives him an alibi. Mr. Brashov was talking to Jamal on the phone at the time of the robbery. He heard Jamal's crying baby. The police finally let Jamal go.

Mr. Brashov and Jamal go to Crossroads Café. Rosa gives Jamal something to eat, but he is not hungry. He is very angry and sad. Jess asks, "What happened out there, Jamal?" Jamal does not want to tell the story. Katherine tells him to file a complaint. Mr. Brashov tells him to forget about it. Jamal says, "Now I know how it feels to be treated badly because of the way you look."

A police officer enters the café with Henry's grandparents. The police officer found them wandering the streets. He helped them find the café. Jess takes them home.

UNIT 10 ◢⊘ LET THE BUYER BEWARE

It's Monday morning. Mr. Brashov is doing paperwork at his desk. Business is not good at Crossroads Café. There are not enough customers. Mr. Brashov is worried.

Later in the afternoon, the café is almost empty. One customer is sitting at the counter. Jess and Mr. Brashov are watching the customer. He asks Katherine for coffee. Then he asks for water. Finally he asks Katherine for her name. He introduces himself. His name is Bill. Katherine isn't very interested in Bill.

An attractive woman comes into the café. She wants to order some dessert. Katherine suggests lemon meringue pie or Mr. Brashov's special apple strudel. The woman orders the apple strudel and she loves it. Mr. Brashov introduces himself to the woman. Her name is Barbara. She is very friendly to Mr. Brashov. Before Barbara leaves the café, she invites Mr. Brashov to have dinner with her.

Mr. Brashov and Barbara go to Palmettos, an expensive restaurant. Barbara tells Mr. Brashov, "I'm a friend of the owner. I helped him win an important award." Barbara helps restaurant owners find customers. She wants to help Mr. Brashov.

Mr. Brashov likes Barbara a lot. They see a lot of each other. Mr. Brashov gives Barbara money to find more customers for Crossroads Café. But Rosa doesn't trust Barbara. She has a bad feeling about her.

Bill asks Katherine to go out for dinner. She says no because she doesn't have a babysitter. Rosa offers to babysit, and Katherine agrees to meet Bill at Palmettos.

The excellent service surprises Katherine. Bill tells her, "My father owns Palmettos." Then Katherine sees Barbara. She is supposed to be out of town, but she is eating dinner with a man. He gives money to Barbara. Katherine gets up quickly and calls Rosa. Katherine tells Bill the problem. Bill thinks of a plan and asks his father for help.

Jamal appears at Palmettos. He has a moustache, and he is dressed like a waiter. He brings a dessert tray to Barbara and her date. Jamal uses a very small camera to take a picture of Barbara and her date.

When the pictures are developed, Katherine shows them to Mr. Brashov. His feelings are hurt and he is angry. He liked Barbara. He also gave her $800 to advertise Crossroads Café.

Mr. Brashov has a plan to get his money back from Barbara. Bill's father, the owner of Palmettos, helps him. First, Mr. Brashov puts an ad in the newspaper for half price lunch specials. Next, he borrows Palmettos's award from Bill's father.

When Barbara comes to the café she is surprised to see so many people. She watches two men in suits give money to Mr. Brashov. Barbara asks Mr. Brashov about them. They are investors, he tells Barbara. He also tells Barbara he won an award.

Barbara wants to invest in the Crossroads's Café, too. Mr. Brashov asks for $900, but he agrees to accept $800.00. After Barbara gives Mr. Brashov the money, he tells her to get out of the café. Barbara screams and yells. Everyone claps when she leaves.

Katherine thanks Bill for his help. Then he asks her for another date. She accepts, on one condition. No restaurants.

It's early in the morning. Mr. Brashov is alone in the café, and he hears a noise. He's worried, but it's Henry. Henry is on his way to school, but he forgot something in his locker. Henry takes everything out of the locker. Finally he finds it—a "how-to" video. It gives instructions about how to operate a video camera. Henry has to make a video for his journalism class at school.

Rosa is tired. She isn't sleeping well because of the water pipes in her apartment. They make a lot of noise. Katherine says, "Maybe you should move."

Rosa saw a "for rent" sign on Katherine's building. She decides to look at the apartment after work. She calls for an appointment. The apartment manager is Katherine's friend.

Rosa meets with Dorothy Walsh, the apartment manager, after work. Rosa loves the apartment. She fills out an application form and gives it to Dorothy. Rosa uses Katherine's name for a reference. Dorothy says, "I'll call you."

Rosa waits for Dorothy to call. She is very anxious and excited about the apartment. Then, Dorothy calls Crossroads Café. Rosa is very happy to hear from her. But Dorothy doesn't give Rosa good news. Dorothy is sorry. She says, "The apartment is rented." Rosa is very disappointed.

Rosa tells everyone about Dorothy's call. Jess doesn't believe Dorothy. He says, "It sounds like discrimination to me." Dorothy is Katherine's friend, so she doesn't agree with Jess.

After work, Katherine talks to Dorothy. Dorothy is showing the apartment to Don Peterson and his daughter, Patty. Katherine is shocked and angry with Dorothy. Dorothy says unkind words about Rosa because she is Mexican.

At work the next day, Katherine tells everyone about Dorothy. Rosa wants to forget about it. But Jess, Jamal, and Henry say no. There are laws against discrimination, but it is hard to prove.

Henry has a plan, and everyone agrees to help him. On Saturday, Henry hides in the empty apartment with his video camera. Then Dorothy comes into the apartment with Don and Patty. She tells them, "You'll be comfortable here. I don't rent to undesirable people."

Suddenly, Mr. Brashov and Jess come into the apartment. Jess wants to rent the apartment. Then Jamal comes in. He wants to rent the apartment, too. Dorothy tells them to leave. She doesn't want their type of people in the building.

Henry comes into view with his camera. He videotaped everything. Now Rosa can prove discrimination. Katherine and Rosa enter the apartment. Dorothy is furious. Katherine tells her, "You and I are no longer friends." Don and Patty decide to look for another apartment.

Dorothy offers the apartment to Rosa. But Rosa doesn't want it anymore. She says, "I don't like the view."

Rosa is going to file a complaint against Dorothy. Katherine will be her witness. And Henry has the proof of discrimination on tape. He will also use the tape for his video project. Henry will call it, *Discrimination in Housing: A Case Study.*

UNIT 12 TURNING POINTS

Mr. Brashov has the key to Crossroads Café in his hand. But the door is already open and there is broken glass on the ground. When he walks into the café, he is shocked. Everything is a mess. The tables and chairs are on the floor. There are broken glasses, bottles, and dishes. There is graffiti on the walls.

Rosa enters the café. At first she doesn't see the mess. Then she tells Mr. Brashov to call the police. Mr. Brashov and Rosa go to the back room. There is more vandalism there. And Mr. Brashov finds a knife with Chinese writing. It is in the wall. Rosa says, "This is the work of a gang."

Mr. Brashov takes the knife from the wall. He thinks the knife belongs to Henry. He will return it to him. Rosa thinks the knife is a message from the gang.

Katherine and Jamal come to work. They are very sad and upset. Mr. Brashov cannot open the café for business. Everyone will work hard to clean the café.

Police Detective Rizzo comes to the café. He agrees with Rosa about the gang. After the detective leaves, Rosa gives the knife to Henry. He is surprised to see it.

Henry is at home. His younger brother Edward and his mother are arguing about Edward's schoolwork. He is not turning in his work on time. Edward complains about his mother to Henry. Edward is very angry with her.

Edward throws darts at a dartboard. Henry throws the knife with Chinese writing at the dartboard. Edward says, "Hey, where did you get that?" Henry doesn't say anything. He just takes the knife and leaves.

Crossroads Café is closed. Katherine and Mr. Brashov are working. The door opens. It's Rosa. She's late to work because the bus was late. Katherine has good news for Rosa. Her neighbor has a used car for sale. If Rosa buys the car, she won't have to take the bus.

Rosa is not excited by Katherine's news. She is embarrassed. Rosa doesn't know how to drive. She has a learner's permit, but she has no time to practice. Jamal and Jess offer to help Rosa.

Henry is talking to Edward at home. Henry asks Edward about the knife. Edward doesn't want to talk. He tries to push Henry out of the way, but Henry throws him to the floor. Edward's shirt rips. Henry sees bruises all over Edward. Finally, Edward talks.

Edward is having problems with a gang. They want him to join. When he tries to avoid them, they beat him. Edward had to give money to the gang. He had to steal from the principal at his school. He had to break into Crossroads Café.

A few days later, a police officer comes into Crossroads Café with Edward. The police officer says, "We think this punk broke into your restaurant. His brother works here." Everyone is shocked. Then the police officer shows Edward's knife to Mr. Brashov. Henry has to tell Mr. Brashov about his brother and the gang.

Mr. Brashov has an idea. Edward and the gang break into Crossroads Café again. But this time, Mr. Brashov is there. And so are all the café employees, people from the neighborhood, and the police. When the police take away the gang, everyone cheers.

UNIT 13 TRADING PLACES

Mr. Brashov is at Crossroads Café. Rosa brings him fish to eat. He is not happy. Mr. Brashov wanted a hamburger and french fries. Rosa wants Mr. Brashov to eat fish. It is better for his health.

Mr. Brashov talks about his dream vacation. First he will drive to Niagara Falls. Then he will camp and fish. But Mr. Brashov cannot take a vacation. He has too much to do at Crossroads Café. If he goes on a vacation, who will manage the café? Jess tells Mr. Brashov to take his dream vacation with his daughter. But Mr. Brashov and his daughter do not get along with each other.

Jess and his wife, Carol, have problems, too. Carol has a job and Jess does not. He is retired. Carol buys Jess a watch, but he is not happy. He thinks it costs too much. They argue about the watch. Carol says she'll return it.

That night, Mr. Brashov thinks about Crossroads Café. He has an idea. The employees should learn each other's jobs. The next day at the café, Mr. Brashov talks about his idea. He wants everyone to change jobs for a day. Today they will watch each other. Tomorrow they will trade places. Rosa will manage the café. Katherine will cook. Henry will wait on the customers. Jamal will deliver the food and bus tables. And Mr. Brashov will be the handyman!

Carol wants to go out to a new restaurant for dinner. Jess says no. It's not Saturday. They can't afford to eat out more than once a week. He will cook dinner. Carol is very unhappy. She thinks Jess has problems because he is not working.

Jess goes to Crossroads Café. It is not open, but Mr. Brashov is still there. He is working late on paperwork. Jess and Mr. Brashov talk about their problems.

The next day everyone trades jobs at the café. At first there are no problems. But at lunchtime, there are a lot of customers and a lot of problems. Mr. Brashov and Jess play chess and watch the employees. Katherine doesn't cook fast enough. Jamal doesn't make a food delivery because he can't find the house. Rosa gives some customers the wrong change. Henry drops some food on the floor.

Carol comes into the café to see Jess. She wants to talk to him about their problems. Carol and Jess argue because of the changes in their lives. They have new roles. They are trading places, too.

Mr. Brashov continues to watch everyone in the café. He is laughing. Then he holds his chest and falls to the ground. Katherine calls 911. Mr. Brashov had a heart attack.

Mr. Brashov had a heart attack. Rosa went to the hospital with him. Now the employees are waiting to hear from Rosa. They are all very nervous and worried.

Finally Rosa calls. Mr. Brashov had a mild heart attack, but now he is out of danger. Everyone wants to visit him at the hospital. But Mr. Brashov cannot have visitors until the next day.

At the hospital, Mr. Brashov is feeling better. He wants to go back to work. Rosa comes to visit. The nurse says, "Mr. Brashov can't have any visitors until tomorrow. The rules are very strict here." But the nurse lets Rosa stay for a few minutes.

Mr. Brashov introduces Rosa to his roommate, Joe Jenkins. Joe Jenkins has heart problems, too. Mr. Jenkins tells Mr. Brashov, "You are a very lucky man. You are in the hospital, but you are alive."

Mr. Brashov argues with his nurse, Brenda. Then Rosa and Mr. Brashov talk about the café. Mr. Brashov is worried, and he wants to close it. Rosa tells Mr. Brashov to take care of himself. The employees will take care of Crossroads Café.

The next day, Rosa opens the café. Soon the other employees come. Rosa tells them what to do. As always, Rosa and Katherine start to argue. Neither of them can work if the other is the boss. Henry is too young to be the boss. Jamal has to take care of his baby, so he cannot be the boss. Then Jess comes. The employees decide he should be the boss. Jess agrees to manage the café until Mr. Brashov returns.

In the hospital, Mr. Brashov complains a lot. Katherine and Henry come to visit. They tell Mr. Brashov about Jess. Jess is a good manager. He has many ideas about how to improve things at the restaurant. But Mr. Brashov is not happy to hear about Jess's ideas. He is worried. Maybe nobody needs him. Everything is fine at the café without him.

When Jamal visits Mr. Brashov, he also talks about Jess. Mr. Brashov is not happy. Jamal brings Mr. Brashov some food from the café. Brenda will not let him eat it. After Jamal leaves, Mr. Brashov is very depressed.

A young woman comes to Crossroads Café. She wants to speak to Jess. Her name is Anna, and she is Mr. Brashov's daughter. She doesn't visit her father in the hospital. She gives Jess a package for him. Then she leaves.

At the hospital, Mr. Brashov continues to feel better, but his roommate, Mr. Jenkins, dies. Mr. Brashov did not know Mr. Jenkins was so sick. He never complained. Mr. Brashov feels very bad because he complains all of the time.

Several days pass. It is late afternoon, and the café is busy. Then the electricity goes out. Nobody knows what to do. Suddenly, they hear Mr. Brashov's voice. He is out of the hospital.

Jess gives Mr. Brashov the package from his daughter, Anna. When Mr. Brashov opens it, he sees a picture of a little girl. It's his granddaughter. Anna never told him about her. Mr. Brashov is very surprised and happy.

UNIT 15 BREAKING AWAY

There are workmen in the vacant building next to Crossroads Café. Mr. Brashov is happy about the new business because vacant buildings are bad for business.

Sara, Henry's girlfriend, comes in the café. Sara says to Henry, "Did you tell them, yet?" Henry finally says, "Sara and I are going together." But nobody is surprised. They already knew.

Sara wants to tell her parents and Henry's parents that they are going together. Henry doesn't think that's necessary. Sara disagrees. She invites Henry to have dinner at her house on Thursday with her parents.

Henry is eating dinner with his parents. His mother has some news. Old friends, the Fongs, are moving back to town. Their daughter, Karen, is the same age as Henry. Karen and Henry played together when they were young. The Fongs are coming for dinner on Thursday night.

Henry says, "I'm having dinner at Sara's on Thursday." Henry's mother tells him to prepare for disappointment. Sara's parents will be unhappy because Henry is Chinese. Henry disagrees with his mother.

Jamal has news for Mr. Brashov. The new business next door is a laundromat. Mr. Brashov doesn't like this news. He thinks a laundromat will be bad for business. People will come to Crossroads Café for change for the laundry machines, not for food.

Rosa suddenly says, "No water!" At the same time, a woman comes in and asks for change for the pay phone. Her name is Linda, and she is the owner of the laundromat. Linda wants to call the Water and Power Company. Her workmen cannot turn off the water to install the washing machines. Mr. Brashov tells her, "Your workmen turned off my water."

It's Thursday night. Henry is having dinner at the Graysons. First, Mr. Grayson talks about football. Henry hates the Graysons' favorite team. Then Henry talks about hockey. The Graysons are not hockey fans. Next, the Graysons talk about food. This is not a good topic either. Finally Henry says, "Sara and I are going together." This is definitely a bad topic.

Sara's mother asks Henry and Sara to wait for a while. Henry thinks Sara's parents don't approve of him. He gets up from the table and leaves the Grayson home.

There are problems at Crossroads Café, too. Mr. Brashov is angry about his new neighbor again. Now her workmen are repainting the lines in the parking lot.

Henry is very sad. He tells Jamal about his dinner at the Graysons and his problems with Sara. Rosa overhears the discussion. Rosa and Katherine give Henry advice. Henry decides to invite his parents, Sara, and her parents to Crossroads Café to talk.

The Changs and the Graysons are at Crossroads Café. Henry apologizes to the Graysons for his rude behavior. Mr. and Mrs. Grayson explain their feelings about Henry and Sara. They talk about their plans for their daughter's future. After a lot of discussion, all of the parents agree to trust their children.

Mr. Brashov decides he likes his new neighbor after all. Linda's workmen made six new parking places—three for him and three for her.

UNIT 16 THE BOTTOM LINE

It's lunchtime on a snowy, winter day. The employees at Crossroads Café are unhappy. The stove is not working, and there are very few customers.

Mr. Brashov is very worried about the stove, and he is angry, too. Jamal tries to fix the stove, but it is very old and needs a new part. Mr. Brashov says, "Maybe I need a new handyman." Jamal's feelings are very hurt.

Jess comes to the café. He usually comes in every day, but yesterday he didn't come. Jess joined a group at the Senior Citizens' Center. Now he plays chess there every morning.

Jess knows about the trouble with the stove. He tells Mr. Brashov to buy a new one. Mr. Brashov has a meeting tomorrow at a bank. He is going to apply for a loan to buy a new stove. Jess gives him advice about how to talk to the banker.

The next day Mr. Brashov goes to the bank. He follows Jess's advice, but it doesn't help. Mr. Littleton, the banker, thinks Mr. Brashov's expenses are too high. He will not approve a loan unless Mr. Brashov cuts his daily costs. One way to do this is to lay off some employees. Mr. Brashov needs to make more money if he wants a loan.

Later at the café, the employees want to know what happened at the bank. Mr. Brashov tells them. They discuss ways to get more customers, so Mr. Brashov can make more money. Henry offers to make flyers for a lunch special. He will put them around the neighborhood.

The next day, Crossroads Café has many customers. Mr. Brashov thanks Henry. But Henry didn't deliver any flyers. He overslept. Jess brought his group from the Senior Citizens' Center to the café for their morning coffee break.

Mr. Littleton from the bank enters the café. At first he is happy to see so many customers. Then he notices something. People are not eating. They are talking, reading the newspaper, playing cards, and sleeping. This is not the way to make more money. He tells Mr. Brashov to make changes fast!

Jess is in Mr. Brashov's office. Mr. Brashov is very sad. He is worried about the café and about the bank loan. Mr. Brashov tells Jess, "The banker thinks I am a fool. He will never give me a loan."

Nobody can find Jamal. Mr. Brashov was angry with Jamal because he couldn't fix the stove. Now Jamal hasn't come to work for two days. The employees wonder, "Is Jamal sick? Is he looking for a new job?"

Jess has another idea for a way to help Mr. Brashov. His seniors group will have lunch and play Bingo at Crossroads Café on Thursday. This time, everybody will order food!

When Mr. Littleton makes another surprise visit to Crossroads Café, he is happy to see so many customers eating. Maybe he will give Mr. Brashov a loan to buy a new stove.

Then Jamal comes to work. He is very dirty, but he is happy. He went to every junkyard in town, and he finally found the part to fix the stove. Mr. Brashov won't need a loan from the bank after all!

UNIT 17 UNITED WE STAND

Rosa is late for work. She is having problems with the water in her apartment. She has green cream on her face, and there is no water to wash her face. Finally, she cleans her face with mouthwash.

At Crossroads Café, Mr. Brashov is worried about Rosa because she is late. The restaurant needs its cook. Jess comes to the restaurant. His back hurts. Jess usually sits at the counter. Mr. Brashov tells him to sit on a chair at a table. The chair will be better for his back.

When Rosa arrives at work, she tells everyone about her water problems. Rosa tries to call the landlord, but she gets the answering machine. Jamal offers to help Rosa. He goes to her apartment after work to look at the pipes. The pipes are very old, and there is a leak. The sink needs a new faucet, too.

While Jamal is fixing the pipe under Rosa's sink, he accidentally breaks Rosa's radio. He takes the broken radio with him so he can fix it.

Rosa is very unhappy about the problems in her apartment building. She decides to write a letter to the building manager. Katherine tries to help. She thinks Rosa's letter is too nice. She gives Rosa suggestions to make the letter stronger. Katherine says, "Say the building is dirty. There are rats everywhere." Rosa is not sure Katherine's suggestions are good ideas.

Jess walks in the cafe. He sees Henry with a video camera. Henry tells Jess, "I'm making a documentary for my class. It's about work." Henry's teacher, Michael McAllister, is a reporter for a local TV station. Henry is filming everyone at the café.

A man comes to Crossroads Café. He is looking for Rosa. He is from the property management company for her building. Rosa did not pay her rent because her apartment needs repairs. Rosa says, "I need some repairs done. My bathroom faucet leaks." The man tells Rosa she must pay, so she gives him a check for the rent. Henry has his video camera, and he films Rosa and the man. This makes the man angry.

Katherine wants to help Rosa. She thinks Rosa should fight for changes in her building. Jess tells Rosa to ask the other tenants for help. Mr. Brashov tells Rosa to have a tenants' meeting at Crossroads Café. Everyone will help her. Jamal will make some signs, and Henry and Katherine will help set up the café for the meeting.

Henry brings Michael McAllister to the meeting. The tenants make a list of all the problems in their building. They elect Rosa president of their group. Then a stranger comes in. His name is Dr. Martinez, and he wants to help the tenants.

The next day at the restaurant, Henry turns on the TV and everyone watches the news. They see a story about the meeting at Crossroads Café. They find out about Dr. Martinez. He invested money in Rosa's building, and he is one of the owners. Before the meeting Dr. Martinez didn't know about the problems. Now he wants to help.

Dr. Martinez comes into the restaurant to see Rosa. He invites her to a meeting with his investment partners. They want to discuss the problems in Rosa's apartment building.

Henry gets his grade for the video. It's a B plus. He didn't get a better grade because his video was not about the topic—work.

Mr. Brashov is looking out the window. Jess asks, "Who are you looking for?" Mr. Brashov says, "Not who, what." Jess then says, "What?" But Mr. Brashov won't tell him. It's a surprise.

Jamal is trying to fix a toaster. He is very unhappy. When Mr. Brashov asks about the toaster, Jamal gets angry.

Mr. Brashov's surprise comes. It's a jukebox. Now Crossroads Café be Crossroads Musical Café! People like to listen to music. Music will bring more customers to Crossroads Café.

Mr. Brashov plugs in the jukebox. Nothing happens. No music. He calls for Jamal. He wants Jamal to fix the jukebox. But Jamal is still angry.

A customer is talking on a cellular phone. He is watching Jamal. He hears Jamal say, "I'm an engineer, not a jukebox engineer." When another customer asks Jamal about the jukebox, Jamal is rude to him. Before the customer with the cellular phone leaves, he gives Jamal his business card. The man's name is Rick Marshall. He owns a construction company. He tells Jamal to call him.

Jamal visits Rick Marshall, and he offers Jamal a job. Mr. Marshall needs a compliance engineer for his company. A compliance engineer makes sure the construction work matches the building plans. Jamal accepts the job.

At the café, Mr. Brashov wants Jamal to make a sign for the café about the jukebox. But Jamal quits his job at Crossroads Café.

Jamal is at the construction company. Mr. Marshall shows Jamal around the job site and introduces him to other employees. Joe Cassidy, a project manager, gives Mr. Marshall an envelope.

Jamal is alone in the construction office at night. The phone rings. He goes to Mr. Marshall's desk to answer the phone. It's Jihan. While Jamal is talking to his wife, he spills some coffee. It falls on an envelope with computer disks.

Jamal is worried about the disks. He wipes the coffee off the disks. Then he puts a disk in the computer to check it for damage. Jamal sees something on the disk. It's a crack in one of the beams for a building at the construction site.

At the café, Mr. Brashov decides to put two ads in the newspaper—one ad is for a handyman and the other ad is for the jukebox. He wants to sell it. The jukebox is too much trouble!

Jamal talks to Mr. Marshall. He wants Jamal to sign some papers. Jamal doesn't want to sign them. He knows the building is not safe. Mr. Marshall gives Jamal an envelope with many one hundred dollar bills in it. It's a bribe to get Jamal to sign the papers. After Mr. Marshall leaves the office, Jamal picks up the telephone. He calls the Department of Building and Safety.

Mr. Brashov is interviewing applicants for the handyman job. He is having no luck finding a new handyman. Then Jamal walks in. He says, "I heard you are looking for a handyman. I'm here to apply for the job."

Jamal is working for Crossroads Café again—not Crossroads Musical Café. Mr. Brashov sold the jukebox.

UNIT 19 THE PEOPLE'S CHOICE

Mr. Brashov is unhappy. There is construction in front of Crossroads Café, and it is keeping customers away. Mr. Brashov calls the city office to complain, but he can't find anyone to speak to.

A young Middle Eastern man enters the café. He tells Mr. Brashov, "People are putting pieces of wood on the street in front of your café." Mr. Brashov doesn't know the man, but he looks familiar.

Jamal enters. He asks, "Has anyone seen my cousin?" The young Middle Eastern man enters the café again. He's Jamal's cousin Hassan. Jamal introduces him to everyone. Hassan likes Rosa very much. Hassan is in the United States to learn English. He wants to be a tour guide in Egypt.

Later that morning, Jess comes to the café. He shows his water bill to Mr. Brashov. Jess's bill for one month of water is $30,000. Jess called the city to complain, but nobody helped him.

Both Jess and Mr. Brashov are unhappy with the city. Mr. Brashov tells Jess to run for city council.

Later at home, Jess talks to his wife, Carol, about Mr. Brashov's idea. Carol thinks it's a good idea, too. She says to Jess, "You could be the *people's choice.*"

Jess decides to run for city council. Crossroads Café becomes his campaign headquarters. There are posters and flyers in the café for Jess Washington, the "People's Choice." But nobody knows Jess, and his name is not mentioned in the newspaper polls.

Mr. Brashov has an idea. He wants Jess to make speeches at Crossroads Café while people are eating. Only one customer is interested in Jess's first speech. His name is Dan Miller.

Dan Miller tells his boss, Mr. Comstock, about Jess. Andrew Comstock is a businessman. He wants to help elect someone to the city council. If Andrew Comstock helps Jess, Jess will help him. Dan brings Mr. Comstock to the café to see Jess.

Dan Miller and Mr. Comstock have a lot of ideas to help Jess. They change his looks, and they give him ideas for speeches. One day, Jess is sitting at a table in Crossroads Café, and nobody recognizes him. Jess is wearing a toupee!

Carol is not happy with the new Jess. She will not vote for him. She doesn't like Mr. Comstock either. He thinks more about money than people.

Jess is giving another speech at Crossroads Café. When Jess sees Carol, he changes his speech. He takes off his toupee. He is the old Jess, and Mr. Comstock is very angry. He won't help Jess anymore.

Hassan is getting ready to return to Egypt. He tries to give Rosa a goat. This is a marriage proposal custom in Egypt. Rosa is very surprised. She likes Hassan, but she doesn't want to marry him.

Election night arrives. Everyone is at Crossroads Café. They are waiting to hear the election results. The phone rings, and Katherine answers it. Jess has 18,706 votes and Tom Johansen has 19,706 votes. Jess didn't win the election, but he didn't lose either.

OUTSIDE LOOKING IN

It's Monday morning. Rosa and Katherine are talking about the weekend. Rosa begins to tell Katherine about a guest teacher. But she is interrupted.

Bill comes to say good-bye to Katherine. He is going to a conference in Chicago. Katherine reminds Bill, "Don't forget my bear." Katherine collects stuffed animals.

Mr. Brashov asks Rosa about lunch. He wants to have a special dessert with lunch because Mr. Shuster, his landlord, is coming to talk about a new lease.

Mr. Shuster tells Mr. Brashov, "You have a wonderful restaurant." Then he gives Mr. Brashov some bad news. The taxes have gone up, and he will probably have to increase the rent.

A man comes into the café. Rosa recognizes him. It's her guest teacher, Andrew Collins. Rosa is very nervous when she talks to Andrew Collins. She tells him about the lunch special. But Mr. Collins doesn't want lunch. He wants to ask Rosa for a favor. Mr. Collins needs a translator for a meeting at his home. Rosa agrees to help him.

Mr. Shuster finishes lunch. Mr. Brashov is nervous about the new lease. He wants to meet with Mr. Shuster and his accountant. But Mr. Shuster is very busy. His son, Stuart, is coming home from school next week. Mr. Shuster's son has to write a school paper about how to run a small business. When Mr. Brashov hears this, he offers to help Stuart.

Rosa is at Andrew Collins' apartment. The furniture is very expensive, and there are a lot of antiques and artwork. One guest, Libby Flanders, is rude to Rosa. She asks Rosa her opinion about a painting. Then she tells Rosa, "You do not belong here."

A few days later at work, Rosa is studying. She's trying to learn about art, music, and wine so she can talk to Andrew and his friends.

Mr. Shuster brings Stuart to Crossroads Café. Mr. Brashov is very surprised. Stuart looks like an 11- or 12-year old. But he dresses and talks like an adult.

Rosa is at Andrew's apartment again. Now she has blond hair, and she talks about art and wine. Andrew is surprised.

At the café, Stuart makes Jamal angry. Jamal and Henry take Stuart out of the café. This worries Mr. Brashov. He calls after them, "You aren't going to do anything violent, are you?"

When Jamal and Henry bring Stuart back to the café, he looks different. His hair is uncombed, and he is dirty. He was playing soccer with Henry and Jamal. Then Mr. Shuster comes in. He's happy about the way Stuart looks. Stuart looks like a kid!

Rosa goes to Andrew's apartment. Andrew is going to Switzerland. Rosa is very disappointed. She enjoyed her dates with Andrew, but they were not dates to him. They were business.

Back at the café, there is one more surprise. Bill is back from Chicago. He kisses Katherine and gives her a big box. Inside, there are two presents, a stuffed bear and an engagement ring.

WALLS AND BRIDGES

Crossroads Café is closed. Mr. Brashov and Rosa are planning menus for the week. María Hernandez comes into the café. She is bringing dinner to her father, César. César is the evening janitor at Crossroads Café. César is also a tailor, and he owns a tailoring shop in the neighborhood.

María shows a photo to Rosa. It is from Big Sister Week at María's school. Rosa is María's "Big Sister," and Rosa is very proud of María. She won a science award at school.

The next day, Mr. Brashov and Jess are playing chess. Jess asks Mr. Brashov about his citizenship exam. Mr. Brashov is studying, but it is very hard. Jess offers to help Mr. Brashov study. But Mr. Brashov refuses Jess's help.

María's teacher, Chris Scanlon comes in the café. She is looking for Rosa. Chris is worried about María because she isn't coming to school anymore. Chris doesn't speak Spanish so she asks Rosa to talk to María's parents.

Rosa goes to the Hernandez's tailoring shop. César is pinning the hem of Rosa's skirt. María is surprised to see Rosa. Rosa tells María about Mrs. Scanlon's visit. María is uncomfortable. Her father doesn't want her to talk to Rosa.

Finally, Rosa asks César, "Why isn't María in school?" César needs María to work in his shop. Rosa is very angry when she hears César's reasons. She wants to do something to help María.

María comes to Crossroads Café to say hello to Rosa. Henry tells María about the work-study program. Students go to school for half a day and work for half a day. Rosa thinks this would be a good way for María to continue school.

Rosa and Mrs. Scanlon go to the tailoring shop. They want to tell Mr. Hernandez about the work-study program. He is not interested. María will get married and have children. She does not need an education.

Mr. Brashov's citizenship test is tomorrow. He can't remember anything. Jess and Katherine offer to help him study. Mr. Brashov finally accepts their help. He also asks Jess to go with him to the interview.

The next day, Mr. Brashov is very excited. He passed the citizenship test. Everyone congratulates him.

Mr. Hernandez comes into the café. Mr. Brashov tells him the news about his citizenship test. Mr. Brashov is very happy, but he is also a little sad. Mr. Brashov's daughter doesn't know about her father's good news. They had a fight, and they don't speak to each other. Mr. Hernandez thinks about Mr. Brashov's problems with his daughter. Mr. Brashov talks about his daughter to Mr. Hernandez.

María comes in the café. She brings her father's dinner. César asks María, "Is it terrible to be a tailor?" María says, "No Papa, not for you." But María doesn't want to be a tailor. She wants to do other things. She wants an education.

Mr. Hernandez surprises María. He finally agrees to talk to Mrs. Scanlon about the work-study program. María can go back to school.

A man is sitting on a bench outside Crossroads Café. He is reading the newspaper. The man needs to shave, and his clothes are dirty.

Henry looks out the window and sees the man. Katherine says, "He's been out there since this morning. Should we do something?" Jess says, "No. He's just reading the paper."

Mr. Brashov is reading a list from Jamal. Jamal is going on vacation so he is leaving some instructions for Mr. Brashov. Jamal and his daughter, Azza, will meet Jihan on a business trip.

Katherine looks out the window again and sees the man on the bench. She asks, "Mr. Brashov, have you noticed that man sitting out front?" She asks Rosa about the man, too. Only Katherine is worried about the man.

Finally, Katherine opens the door for Jess. The man is at the door. His hands are in his pockets. Katherine asks the man, "What do you want?" He says, "I need something to eat." The man comes into the café. Katherine thinks the man is a robber with a gun. She tells Rosa to make a turkey sandwich for him, quickly.

The man is very nervous. He starts to take his hands out of his pockets. Everyone puts their hands in the air. The man is very confused. He is not a robber. He is just hungry.

The lights go out in the café. The man helps Mr. Brashov fix the lights. Then he introduces himself. His name is Frank. He has not worked for 18 months. Mr. Brashov and Jess want to help him. Katherine does not. She doesn't trust Frank.

The next day at the café, Mr. Brashov is trying to fix a lock. Then Frank comes in and offers to help. Mr. Brashov asks Frank to fill in for Jamal. Frank is the new handyman for a week.

Jess is having car problems. Frank offers to look at Jess's car. Frank used to be a mechanic. When Jess tries to pay Frank, Frank refuses the money.

Jess wants to help Frank. Jess used to work at the post office. He knows about a job there, so he sets up a job interview for Frank.

Frank has good job skills, but he doesn't do well on job interviews. Jess and Mr. Brashov help Frank get ready for the interview. They pretend to interview him. Henry types his resumé. Rosa gives him a shave, and Jess gives him some clothes. Finally, Frank is ready for his job interview.

Jess's friend, Marty, comes to Crossroads Café to interview Frank. Frank is very nervous. He gives Marty his resumé. They talk for a little bit, but then Frank gets up and walks away.

Frank feels very bad. He disappointed Jess and Mr. Brashov. Katherine talks to Frank. She tells him, "I know how you feel. When I came to Crossroads Café, I was very nervous, too."

Katherine gives Frank some advice. She tells him to imagine the interviewer is in his underwear. Then Frank won't be so nervous.

Frank gets another chance to interview with Marty. This time he follows Katherine's advice, and he gets the job!

UNIT 23 THE GIFT

Katherine, Rosa, and Jamal are in the café. Katherine and Rosa are organizing things for a party.

Mr. Brashov arrives. "What a beautiful day," he says. Rosa says, "It's a very special day." Mr. Brashov is happy. He thinks Rosa remembered his birthday. But Rosa doesn't say, "Happy Birthday." She says, "Today is special because Jamal is going to fix the ice maker." Mr. Brashov is very sad. Nobody remembered his birthday.

A customer comes in the café. His name is Joe. Mr. Brashov hasn't seen Joe for awhile. Joe was at his son's cabin in the mountains. Joe shows Mr. Brashov some pictures. He tells Mr. Brashov to take a vacation.

Jamal is in the utility room. He is putting party decorations in his locker. Mr. Brashov walks in. Jamal tries to hide what he is doing. He doesn't want Mr. Brashov to know about the party. Fortunately, the phone rings. Mr. Brashov picks up the phone and says hello. But no one answers.

Joe comes back to the café with the keys to his son's cabin. He invites Mr. Brashov to the cabin. It's only two hours away. Mr. Brashov can go after work. When Katherine and Rose hear this, they are worried. If Mr. Brashov goes to the cabin, he will miss the surprise birthday party. Mr. Brashov leaves the café with Joe.

Jess and Katherine are in the utility room. Jess is typing a letter from the Internal Revenue Service (IRS) to give to Mr. Brashov. When Mr. Brashov returns to the café, Katherine gives him the mail.

Mr. Brashov sees a letter from the IRS. Someone from the IRS is coming to the café on Monday to see Mr. Brashov's tax records. Now Mr. Brashov cannot go to the cabin.

Jess has a solution to the problem. Mr. Brashov can call Emery Bradford to help him. If Emery and Mr. Brashov work on the tax records tonight, Mr. Brashov can go to the cabin on Saturday.

Emery comes to the café. Mr. Brashov is very depressed. This is not a very happy birthday for him. The phone rings again. It's Nicolae. He's calling to say "Happy Birthday" to his brother.

Mr. Brashov hangs up the phone. He calls information to get the number for the airport. He leaves the café. When Emery looks for Mr. Brashov, he can't find him. The door to the café opens. Everyone is there for Mr. Brashov's surprise party. But Mr. Brashov is not there!

Mr. Brashov is at the airport. His daughter, Anna, works at the ticket counter. She is very surprised to see her father. She hasn't seen him for a long time. Anna and Mr. Brashov talk.

Suddenly, Mr. Brashov sees his friends from the café. They want Mr. Brashov to return to the café for his surprise birthday party. Jess invites Anna to come, too, but she says she can't.

Back at the café, Mr. Brashov finally celebrates his birthday. There is a cake and gifts. And one gift is very special. Anna comes to the café—with her daughter, Elizabeth. For the first time, Mr. Brashov meets his granddaughter. Mr. Brashov finally has a very happy birthday.

UNIT 24 ALL'S WELL THAT ENDS WELL

It's snowing and Crossroads Café is closed. Jamal, Henry, Mr. Brashov, and Jess are looking at their watches. Rosa has a clipboard. She says to the men, "Let's synchronize our watches." Mr. Brashov and Rosa are having a dinner party for Katherine and Bill in four hours, forty-five minutes, and seventeen seconds. They are getting married tomorrow.

Everyone has a job to do except Henry. Mr. Brashov is making beef stroganoff. Jamal is putting up decorations. Carol is picking up the flowers.

A delivery man comes in the café with a box for Katherine. It's her wedding dress. Rosa opens the box to check on the dress. Oh no! The dress is the wrong size. It's huge. It's big enough for two or three Katherines to wear. Henry says, "Katherine had better start eating."

Henry goes outside to check the weather. It's snowing very hard. Rosa is worried about Katherine's grandfather. He is flying in from Europe, and someone has to pick him up at the airport.

There is another problem. Rosa hears Suzanne and David arguing in the kitchen. They were helping Rosa make pastries and Suzanne lost her mother's wedding ring!

Katherine and Bill enter the café. They are very happy. But when Katherine greets her children, Suzanne starts to cry and runs out of the room.

Everyone tells Katherine about the problems. Katherine is not happy any more. She asks about her wedding dress and decides to try it on. Katherine locks herself in the bathroom and cries after she sees the dress. She won't talk to anyone. She just cries.

Mr. Brashov tries to call the airport for information about flights from Europe. Everyone, except for Katherine, is listening to the radio. The weather is getting worse.

Finally, there is a job for Henry. Mr. Brashov decides to send Henry to the airport to pick up Katherine's grandfather. He gives Henry money for a taxi. Katherine gives Henry a description of her grandfather so Henry will recognize him.

Bill's family starts to arrive at the café for the dinner party. Bill's Uncle Antonio sees Rosa and calls her Katherine. He welcomes her to the family. Rosa is so surprised, she can't speak.

Henry has several problems at the airport. First, he picks up the wrong man. Then he finds the right man, but the taxi has a flat tire on the way back to Crossroads Café. Katherine's grandfather changes the tire.

Back at the café, Bill tells his family Rosa is not Katherine. Jamal says, "Katherine is at home. She's checking on her wedding dress." Bill's family doesn't know Katherine is in the utility room. She is a mess because she is crying.

Jamal helps Katherine climb out a window. Then she enters the café again— through the front door. Everyone is very happy to finally meet the bride!

The bride is happy, too. Her grandfather comes in with Henry and the taxi driver, and the party begins. When they all sit down to eat, Aunt Sophie finds the missing wedding ring in a pastry. All's well that ends well!

Rosa is speaking Spanish to some customers. When Katherine comes to take their order, she speaks Spanish, too. Rosa says, "Congratulations. I almost understood you."

Jamal asks Katherine about her plans for the future. Katherine is leaving Crossroads Café to spend time with her children, help her husband, and go back to school. Katherine wants to be a lawyer. Rosa laughs and says, "That is a perfect job for you!"

Mr. Brashov has one last task for Katherine. He wants her to hire the new waitress. This worries Rosa.

Henry is in the office of a record producer, Danny. Henry wants to be a rock star. The producer listens to a tape of Henry and his band. They sound good, but the producer wants to hear them play in person. Henry invites Danny to a live concert at Crossroads Café.

The next day at the café, Jamal gets a phone call. It's a friend from Egypt. Jamal's friend, Abdullah, is in town and Jamal invites him for dinner.

Katherine interviews waitresses. She talks to many applicants, but she doesn't hire anyone. Rosa, Jess, and Mr. Brashov don't understand Katherine. There are many qualified people, but Katherine is still looking.

Jess wants to play chess with Mr. Brashov, but Mr. Brashov has too much work to do. He promises to play chess with Jess on Friday.

Henry tells Katherine about Danny. He is coming to Crossroads Café to hear Henry play. There's only one problem. Henry has to ask Mr. Brashov for permission to have a concert at the café. Mr. Brashov is not enthusiastic, but he agrees.

It's night. Jamal is eating dinner at home with Abdullah, his friend from Egypt. Abdullah's company needs a chief engineer. Abdullah offers Jamal a job in Egypt.

Jihan is surprised to learn Jamal wants to return to Egypt. Jihan likes her job, and she is happy in the United States. But Jamal is unhappy. He used to be an engineer, and now he is a handyman. Jamal doesn't want to be a handyman anymore.

The next day, Katherine interviews another applicant for the waitress job, a young Haitian woman, Marie. Rosa asks Katherine, "How was she?" Katherine answers, "Great." But Katherine didn't hire Marie. Katherine's looking for the perfect waitress.

Later in the evening, there is a crowd at the café. Danny, the producer , comes to hear Henry and the band. Henry is happy to see Danny there. But the next day, when he goes to see Danny, Henry is very disappointed. Danny doesn't think Henry is good enough to sign a contract. Danny tells Henry to go to college.

It's Katherine's last day at Crossroads Café. And surprise—the café finally has a new waitress—Marie. Katherine introduces Jess to Marie. Then Jess and Mr. Brashov start to play chess. A delivery man interrupts their game. Jess is disappointed. Mr. Brashov promises to finish the game after Katherine's party.

The café is closed for the day, and the party for Katherine begins. Everyone is there except Carol and Jess. Then the phone rings. It's Carol. She has terrible news. Jess was in a car accident. Jess is dead. Katherine's party is over.

WINDS OF CHANGE

It's early afternoon at Crossroads Café, and Mr. Brashov is thinking about Jess. Mr. Brashov misses Jess a lot.

Jihan comes in the café to see Jamal. Jihan tells Jamal, "I have found a company to ship our things to Egypt." Jamal surprises Jihan when he says, "I don't think we should move back to Egypt." They discuss their decision to return to Egypt, and finally, Jihan agrees with Jamal. They will stay in the United States.

Carol Washington is at home with her son, Daryl. Someone knocks at the door. It's Mr. Brashov. He is holding a shopping bag. Mr. Brashov has something for Carol. It's a chess board—the one he and Jess used to play chess.

Carol shows Mr. Brashov an envelope with tickets for a cruise to the Greek Islands. She wanted to surprise Jess on their anniversary, but now Jess is gone. When Mr. Brashov leaves, Carol cries.

Katherine makes a surprise visit to the café. She shows Rosa a catalogue from City College. Henry stops working to talk to Katherine, too. But Marie tells him to get back to work.

A few minutes later, Henry has an accident. His hand is bleeding. While Marie helps Henry, Katherine waits on the customers. Henry tells Marie, "You should have been a nurse." Marie tells Henry, "I am."

Marie was a nurse in Haiti. She has to go back to school before she can be a nurse in the United States. Henry doesn't like to talk about going to school. He wants to be a rock star, not a student. Marie advises Henry to go to college.

Carol Washington comes in the café to talk to Mr. Brashov. This time Carol has something for Mr. Brashov. She gives him the tickets for the cruise to the Greek Islands. At first, Mr. Brashov doesn't want to accept the tickets. But finally he takes them—for Jess.

A few days later, Mr. Brashov walks around the café with a businessman, Mr. Clayborne. When Mr. Clayborne leaves, Mr. Brashov surprises everyone. He tells them "Mr. Clayborne is the new owner of Crossroads Café. I am 65-years old, and I want to enjoy my life."

It's a week later. The café is closed, but Mr. Brashov and Mr. Clayborne are talking. Jamal comes in with a box and news for Mr. Brashov. He and Jihan changed their minds again. This time they have definitely decided to return to Egypt. Mr. Clayborne also has news for Mr. Brashov. He will bring his own employees to Crossroads Café.

Jamal stops to talk to Henry, Rosa, and Marie. Henry has some news, too. He is going to go to college. Jamal congratulates Henry.

A few minutes later, Mr. Brashov says good-bye to Mr. Clayborne. Now it is Mr. Brashov's turn to give Rosa some news. Mr. Clayborne is not going to be the owner of Crossroads Café. Mr. Brashov has decided to keep the café and hire a manager. The new manager is Rosa Rivera!